DISEASES & DISORDERS

Brain Trauma

Hal Marcovitz

LUCENT BOOKS

A part of Gale, Cengage Learning

GALE
CENGAGE Learning

Detroit • New York • San Francisco • New Haven, Conn • Waterville, Maine • London

LIBRARY OF CONGRESS CATALOGING-IN-PUBLICATION DATA

Marcovitz, Hal.
 Brain trauma / By Hal Marcovitz.
   p. cm. — (Diseases & disorders)
 Includes bibliographical references and index.
 ISBN 978-1-4205-0112-4 (hardcover)
 1. Brain damage—Popular works. I. Title.
 RC387.5.M368 2009
 617.4'81044—dc22

                                        2008046533

Lucent Books
27500 Drake Rd.
Farmington Hills, MI 48331

ISBN-13: 978-1-4205-0112-4
ISBN-10: 1-4205-0112-7

Printed in the United States of America
2 3 4 5 6 7 13 12 11 10 09

Table of Contents

Foreword 4

Introduction
Brain Trauma: The Invisible Epidemic 6

Chapter One
What Is Brain Trauma? 10

Chapter Two
How Do Brains Get Traumatized? 25

Chapter Three
Living with Brain Trauma 40

Chapter Four
Treating and Preventing Brain Trauma 56

Chapter Five
The Future of Brain Trauma 72

Notes 87
Glossary 92
Organizations to Contact 94
For Further Reading 97
Index 100
Picture Credits 104
About the Author 104

"The Most Difficult Puzzles Ever Devised"

Charles Best, one of the pioneers in the search for a cure for diabetes, once explained what it is about medical research that intrigued him so. "It's not just the gratification of knowing one is helping people," he confided, "although that probably is a more heroic and selfless motivation. Those feelings may enter in, but truly, what I find best is the feeling of going toe to toe with nature, of trying to solve the most difficult puzzles ever devised. The answers are there somewhere, those keys that will solve the puzzle and make the patient well. But how will those keys be found?"

Since the dawn of civilization, nothing has so puzzled people—and often frightened them, as well—as the onset of illness in a body or mind that had seemed healthy before. A seizure, the inability of a heart to pump, the sudden deterioration of muscle tone in a small child—being unable to reverse such conditions or even to understand why they occur was unspeakably frustrating to healers. Even before there were names for such conditions, even before they were understood at all, each was a reminder of how complex the human body was, and how vulnerable.

While our grappling with understanding diseases has been frustrating at times, it has also provided some of humankind's most heroic accomplishments. Alexander Fleming's accidental discovery in 1928 of a mold that could be turned into penicillin has resulted in the saving of untold millions of lives. The isolation of the enzyme insulin has reversed what was once a death sentence for anyone with diabetes. There have been great strides in combating conditions for which there is not yet a cure, too. Medicines can help AIDS patients live longer, diagnostic tools such as mammography and ultrasounds can help doctors find tumors while they are treatable, and laser surgery techniques have made the most intricate, minute operations routine.

This "toe-to-toe" competition with diseases and disorders is even more remarkable when seen in a historical continuum. An astonishing amount of progress has been made in a very short time. Just two hundred years ago, the existence of germs as a cause of some diseases was unknown. In fact, it was less than 150 years ago that a British surgeon named Joseph Lister had difficulty persuading his fellow doctors that washing their hands before delivering a baby might increase the chances of a healthy delivery (especially if they had just attended to a diseased patient)!

Each book in Lucent's Diseases and Disorders series explores a disease or disorder and the knowledge that has been accumulated (or discarded) by doctors through the years. Each book also examines the tools used for pinpointing a diagnosis, as well as the various means that are used to treat or cure a disease. Finally, new ideas are presented—techniques or medicines that may be on the horizon.

Frustration and disappointment are still part of medicine, for not every disease or condition can be cured or prevented. But the limitations of knowledge are being pushed outward constantly; the "most difficult puzzles ever devised" are finding challengers every day.

Brain Trauma: The Invisible Epidemic

Each year, more than 1.5 million Americans sustain traumatic brain injuries, caused mostly by motor vehicle accidents, falls and similar mishaps, violence, and sports injuries. Such injuries can be as mild as a concussion or as severe as having a foreign object, such as a shard from a broken window, penetrate the skull and lodge in brain tissue. The more serious the injury, the more likely it will cause permanent brain damage which can impair the victim's ability to speak, think clearly, or otherwise function normally. In the most traumatic cases, head injuries can be deadly.

The risk of traumatic brain injury, or TBI, is particularly high among young people because this age group is more likely to engage in activities and behaviors that expose them to head injuries. Adolescent boys, for example, are very prone to TBI because they often ride bicycles or motorbikes without helmets or participate in contact sports. Many young people do not even perceive the risks of head injuries when performing wild stunts or playing a hard-hitting football game.

George Zitnay, a neuropsychologist who treats people with mental illnesses that result from brain injuries, calls TBI an "invisible epidemic"[1] because the American public knows little about them. He also claims that mental disability is often stigmatized in our society, so many people don't know how to deal with the consequences of brain injuries and even turn away from those who suffer them. "You get a brain injury in this country, you keep it quiet because here we value intellect so much," Zitnay says. "It's a very frightening thing to think about the psyche, to think about the mind. If you were brain injured, would you want people to know about it?"[2]

The Sad Saga of Andre Waters

Sometimes, it is immediately evident that someone has suffered a brain injury. Paramedics who arrive at the scene of an auto accident usually can quickly determine whether the victim's head has been injured. Likewise, doctors or trainers who respond to an injury on a football field quickly suspect brain trauma if the player is confused, glassy-eyed, suffering from neck pain, or exhibiting other symptoms that make it clear he took a blow to the head.

In other cases, though, it may take weeks, months, or even years before the effects of brain trauma appear. Andre Waters is one well-publicized example. Waters played professional football for eleven years, earning a reputation as one of the National Football League's (NFL) hardest-hitting defenders. During his career, Waters suffered numerous concussions, which are bruises to the brain. He once told a reporter, "I think I lost count at fifteen. I just wouldn't say anything. I'd sniff some smelling salts, then go back in there."[3]

After retiring from pro football, Waters held a number of coaching jobs at small colleges. Throughout his life, Waters had been an amiable, friendly, and outgoing person, but his failure to find a coaching job with an NFL team clearly troubled him. Each year, his friends and family members noticed that he was growing more distant and depressed. Finally, in late 2006, Waters committed suicide at the age of forty-four.

After his death, an autopsy concluded that Waters's brain resembled that of an eighty-year-old patient afflicted with Alzheimer's disease, a progressive brain disorder that affects mostly people over age sixty-five, associated with loss

It wasn't discovered that Andre Waters was suffering from brain trauma until after his death.

of memory and other cognitive abilities, mood swings, and ultimately dementia. According to physicians, the numerous concussions Waters suffered throughout his career caused the condition and was also responsible for his depression and suicidal tendencies. Said Chris Nowinski, a former professional wrestler and now an author and advocate for athletes with brain damage, "I can only imagine with that much physical damage in your brain, what that must have felt like for him."[4]

"Tired and Numb"

Throughout his career, Waters ignored the symptoms of brain trauma and kept returning to the field. Other athletes have heeded their doctors' advice, giving up their playing careers rather than risking the long-term consequences of brain trauma. Among the professional football players who have retired early with a history of head injury are Steve Young, Troy Aikman, Wayne Chrebet, Al Toon, Bill Romanowski, Ed McCaffrey, Chris Miller, Stan Humphries, Dan Morgan, and Merril Hoge. All suffered numerous concussions on the playing field.

Hoge spent eight seasons in the NFL as a fullback for the Pittsburgh Steelers and Chicago Bears. As a fullback, Hoge's primary responsibility was to block for the halfback—to throw his body into bigger linemen, clearing the way for the ball carrier to gain yards up the field. It is a gritty, physical position that requires the player to sacrifice his body and endure pain for the good of the team.

In 1994 Hoge suffered a concussion while playing for the Bears. He left the game but days later showed up for practice to prepare for the next game on the schedule, even though he still felt groggy and lightheaded. The following Sunday, Hoge took the field and found himself unable to remember the plays. He also suffered another concussion. "I went to the locker room and actually stopped breathing," he recalled. "They thought they lost me. I spent two weeks in the intensive care unit, and then I spent thirteen months just trying to relearn how to read, how to drive. For those thirteen months I had no drive and no feeling—I was just tired and numb."[5]

Even after all that, Hoge hoped to return to his team but was unable to convince a doctor to clear him to play. Reluctantly, Hoge retired from football. In 2006 Hoge said that if he had known as much about concussions then as he does now, he would have retired much earlier in his career: "Someone should absolutely be telling [players] about the links they've found between multiple concussions and Alzheimer's disease, depression and those other problems, and that each concussion increases [the] risk. We do that with hips and knees all the time, except you can replace hips and knees. You can't replace the brain."[6]

The examples of Waters, Hoge, and many others illustrate how TBI can alter people's lives. While their cases have become well known because of their status as celebrities, across America thousands of people out of the spotlight live with disabilities caused by traumatic brain injury. Even such simple, routine tasks as brushing their teeth, riding a bus, and reading a book become challenges as they adjust to daily life at home and at work following traumatic brain injuries.

CHAPTER ONE

What Is Brain Trauma?

A traumatic brain injury is any injury sustained to the head that disrupts the functions of the brain. A mild form of brain trauma, such as a concussion, results in a temporary disruption of mental stability and may bring about a brief period of disorientation, dizziness, or loss of consciousness. Much more severe cases of brain trauma can result in extended periods of unconsciousness. Depending on the extent of the injury, a victim may lapse into a coma for days, months, or longer. Even after regaining consciousness, people who have experienced severe brain trauma may suffer from other long-term problems such as amnesia—the partial or complete loss of memory. Many find their cognitive and motor functions are impaired—they may be unable to communicate or think coherently, and the body's normal reactions to stimuli may be confused.

"A tap on the head, and anything can go wrong," says author and social worker Michael Paul Mason, who assists survivors of brain trauma:

> Anything usually does go wrong. You may not remember how to swallow. Or you may look at food and perspire instead of salivate, or salivate when you hear your favorite song. You may not know your name, or you may think you're someone different every hour. Everyone you know

and will ever know could become a stranger, including the face in the mirror.[7]

Doctors classify brain trauma in two categories: closed head injuries and open head injuries. As the names suggest, a closed head injury involves trauma in which the skull remains intact, while an open head injury involves a direct and forceful impact on the skull hard enough to break it open. Certainly, open head injuries are regarded as extremely serious, but closed head injuries can also be devastating.

An X-ray shows a brain injury to the back of the head. Brain trauma is classified in two categories: closed head injuries and open head injuries.

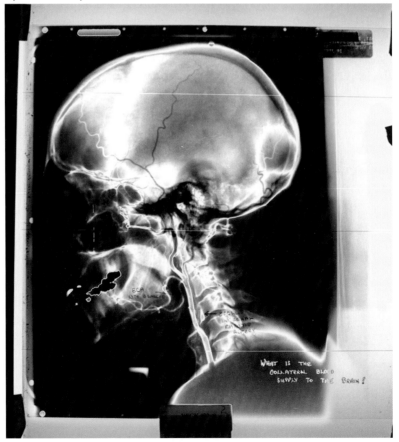

Closed Head Injuries

The brain is the body's most complicated organ. Its tissue is composed of billions of cells that work in concert to enable people to think, learn, speak, see, take steps, manipulate eating utensils and tools, and carry out hundreds of other functions. When the brain is damaged, it may no longer be able to provide the rest of the body with the instructions to perform even the simplest of tasks.

Several significant anatomical features have evolved to protect this most complex vital organ against injury. The most obvious is the bony skull that encases the brain; the average adult skull is from 6.5 to 7.1 millimeters thick, or a little more than a quarter-inch thick. Inside the skull, the brain is surrounded by the meninges—three layers of tissue and fluid that act as padding. The skull and meninges are tough and resilient, but they can't ensure absolute protection. They can't stop a bullet or glass shard from penetrating the brain. A significant blow to the head can cause a skull fracture. Even a fall off a bicycle can damage these protective layers and the brain within.

Brain cells, or neurons, communicate with one another through structures called axons and dendrites. The axon is a fiber that extends from the nucleus of the cell; it splits into a network of smaller fibers known as dendrites. The dendrites from one neuron do not quite connect to the dendrites of the next neuron; there is a tiny gap, or synapse, that is bridged by electrical impulses. When the head sustains a blow, parts of the brain may shift inside the skull while other parts remain stable. This movement tears, stretches, and twists the axons and dendrites. "Imagine that you have an electric cable made up of individual wires," says Lance Trexler, director of rehabilitation neuropsychology at the Rehabilitation Hospital of Indiana. "If you hit that cable with a hammer, the wires would break."[8]

Those twisted and damaged axons and dendrites—a sort of biological "faulty wiring"—cause a brain trauma patient to exhibit a variety of symptoms, including blurry or double vision, difficulty concentrating, inability to swallow, dizziness, headache, poor coordination, lightheadedness, loss of balance,

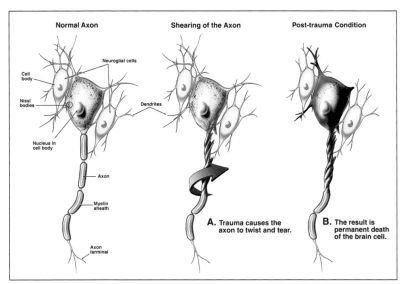

Normal Axon   Shearing of the Axon   Post-trauma Condition

Neuroglial cells

Cell body

Nissl bodies

Dendrites

Nucleus in cell body

Axon

Myelin sheath

Axon terminal

A. Trauma causes the axon to twist and tear.

B. The result is permanent death of the brain cell.

This illustration shows the stages of an axon shear. The axon is a fiber that extends from the nucleus of the cell.

loss of memory, muscle stiffness or spasms, seizures, slurred or slow speech, tingling or numbness, pain, a sense of spinning known as vertigo, and muscle weakness in the limbs or other parts of the body.

Brain trauma patients typically experience these symptoms soon after the mishap that caused their injuries. If the injury occurs during a traffic accident or other public incident, the patient may be transported to a hospital emergency room. In such circumstances, paramedics, physicians, and nurses are trained to look for brain trauma symptoms immediately. However, if the mishap occurs at home, the victim may just shake off the injury, thinking it is not serious. Other, delayed symptoms may show up days or weeks later, including anxiety or nervousness, behavioral changes, depression, and insomnia.

Ignoring the Symptoms

The danger of ignoring the immediate symptoms of brain trauma is that, though it may not be obvious at first, severe damage may have occurred. Blood vessels in the brain can rupture, causing bleeding in the brain. That will make the brain tissue

Grading Concussions

Some sports-related concussions are more serious than others. To guide doctors who treat athletes, the American Academy of Neurology has categorized concussions as Grade 1 (minor), Grade 2 (moderate), and Grade 3 (severe).

In a Grade 1 concussion there is no loss of consciousness, but the athlete displays a degree of confusion that lasts less than fifteen minutes. Athletes who sustain Grade 1 concussions can return to the field, but if they suffer a second Grade 1 concussion during the game, they are typically pulled out of competition and benched until they have been symptom-free for a week.

In a Grade 2 concussion, there is no loss of consciousness, but the athlete displays confusion for more than fifteen minutes. Athletes who suffer a Grade 2 concussion are routinely taken out of the game and benched until they have been symptom-free for a week. If their symptoms persist for more than a week, they often undergo further tests.

In a Grade 3 concussion, the athlete has suffered a loss of consciousness. Grade 3 patients are taken out of the game and benched until symptom-free for a week if their unconsciousness spanned a few seconds, longer if they were out for a few minutes. If tests show brain swelling or other symptoms, the athlete commonly is benched for the season and urged to give up contact sports.

swell, building up pressure inside the skull. When the brain is under pressure, the supply of oxygen to the neurons may be cut off, killing brain cells. Also, the pressure may force the brain downward, destroying cells at the base of the brain.

You would think that people would naturally seek medical treatment for severe headaches, dizziness, double vision, and the other symptoms of brain trauma, but ignoring such symptoms is actually quite common, especially in contact sports. For example, Willie Baun, a Manchester, Massachusetts, seventh-grader, took what seemed to be an ordinary hit while playing football. Feeling woozy, he came out of the game. Baun sat on the bench for two games, then played again—even though he was still experiencing headaches. During his first game back with the team, he sustained another blow to the head. Doctors later diagnosed both blows as concussions.

After a concussion, calcium builds up in brain cells as they chemically react to the trauma. Calcium is an essential mineral in the human body, a main part of the structure of bones and teeth. It can also be found in neurons, where it is a vital part of the electrical activity that transmits signals from neuron to neuron. However, a calcium buildup in the neurons can be toxic to the brain cells. When there is too much calcium in the brain cells, the neurons stop working properly. If the patient rests and avoids further trauma, his or her brain cells can eventually rid themselves of their excess calcium through the normal process of electrical transmission. But if the neurons undergo further trauma before they have recovered, there can be an even further buildup of calcium.

Studies have shown that people who have received one concussion are more likely to sustain a concussion in the future. Even when the symptoms of concussion have completely resolved between injuries, people who receive a series of minor head blows over time—such as boxers, football and hockey players, and young athletes—risk developing repetitive head injury syndrome, the slow decline of cognitive abilities.

The risk of serious impairment goes up if a person suffers a second concussion before the brain has recovered from an initial concussion. In rare cases, even a mild second concussion can cause rapid, out-of-control brain swelling, a life-threatening condition known as second-impact syndrome, or SIS. Half of SIS cases are fatal, and those who have survived SIS are severely disabled.

Though Willie Baun fortunately did not develop SIS, he suffered temporary amnesia—he had trouble recognizing his parents and friends, and could read and do math on a second-grade level only. It took eight months before Baun's symptoms cleared up and he was able to perform again at a middle school level. Looking back, Baun says he was wrong to ignore the symptoms of his concussion. "Even people who know my story think it can't happen to them," he says. "They have to be honest with doctors and parents that maybe they're having symptoms. Maybe they're not all right."[9]

Blood Clots on the Brain

The concussion is the most common form of TBI. Of the 1.5 million cases of brain trauma that occur each year, about 75 percent are diagnosed as concussions. Simply a bruise to the brain, a concussion might involve a brief period of headache, nausea, fatigue, confusion, sleep disturbance, and memory lapses before the patient recovers. However, some patients continue to experience symptoms for several days or weeks before returning to normal. As the cases of Andre Waters and Willie Baun prove, more than one concussion can lead to more severe, long-term consequences.

There are many forms of closed head trauma that are far more serious than a concussion. Among them are an infarction, which is also known as a stroke. An infarction occurs when blood is cut off to the brain, preventing oxygen from reaching brain cells. Most strokes are suffered by elderly people or patients with heart conditions that cause a reduction in blood flow through the brain. However, TBI can also cause infarctions by compressing a blood vessel in the brain, cutting off vital blood supply. Depending on where in the brain it occurs, stroke can cause varying degrees of paralysis or speech and memory impairment, and a major stroke can rapidly lead to coma or death.

A blow to the head also could cause internal bleeding. This condition is known as a hemorrhage—bleeding in the brain that occurs when blood leaks from a damaged vessel. In most cases, bleeding occurs within minutes of the injury, but sometimes it may not start for several hours. The consequences of a brain hemorrhage are like those of a stroke.

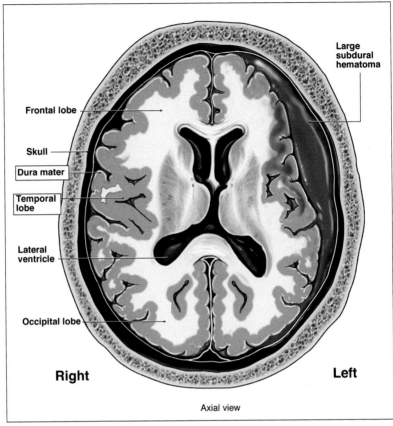

Large subdural hematoma

Frontal lobe

Skull

Dura mater

Temporal lobe

Lateral ventricle

Occipital lobe

Right

Left

Axial view

This illustration shows a subdural hematoma of the brain, which is bleeding inside the skull but not actually in the brain.

Another form of bleeding caused by TBI is known as a subdural hematoma—bleeding inside the skull but not actually in the brain. Subdural hematomas increase pressure inside the skull to often dangerous levels. Also, when cranial bleeding dries it forms what is known as a clot, which is a mass of hardened blood. The clot itself exerts pressure on the sensitive brain tissue. Hematomas and clots can block blood vessels, leading to stroke, or damage brain cells by their own pressure, leading to permanent impairment of brain function.

That is what happened to lightweight boxing champ Leavander Johnson, who took a tremendous beating from his opponent while defending his title in a September 2005 nationally

The Glasgow Coma Scale

When a brain injury patient arrives in the emergency room, a doctor will attempt to assess the degree of the trauma by asking the patient several questions, such as "What is your name?" and "What day is it?" and by asking the patient to perform a series of simple movements, such as wiggling toes or opening and closing eyes. The doctor pays close attention to the patient's responses, rating the person's consciousness on a commonly accepted numeric scale known as the Glasgow Coma Scale, or GCS.

For example, the patient's ability to open his or her eyes is ranked from 1 to 4. A score of 4 means the patient spontaneously opens his or her eyes; opening the eyes in response to painful stimuli is scored as 2; no response at all is scored as 1. Similar assessments are made for verbal responses (on a scale of 1 to 5) and motor responses (on a scale of 1 to 6). If, for example, the patient can converse clearly and spontaneously, the doctor rates the patient a 5 on the verbal scale; if the patient replies with incomprehensible sounds, the doctor will give the patient a 2. If no response is given, the doctor will grade the patient with a 1.

Obviously, the patients who score the lowest on the GCS are suffering from the most severe forms of brain injury and are in need of immediate medical attention, such as surgery. A total score of 8 or below (out of a possible 15) indicates the patient is in a coma.

televised match. Johnson stayed on his feet despite punches to his head, but the referee finally stopped the fight in the eleventh round. Johnson returned to his dressing room under his own power, then complained of a headache and collapsed. Doctors diagnosed a cranial hematoma and clot; Johnson underwent emergency surgery to remove the clot and relieve the pressure inside his skull, but the damage was too severe. In a coma, his condition deteriorated and he died five days later after his family agreed to remove life support.

Observers believe Johnson may have survived had he not been so willing to take punishment in what was obviously a losing battle in the ring. "This kid's courage was his downfall,"[10] said boxing promoter Lou DiBella.

Soon after Johnson's death another boxer, heavyweight Joe Mesi, suffered a hematoma that kept him out of boxing for two years. Against the advice of doctors and fight experts, Mesi elected to fight again. Said boxing analyst Teddy Atlas, "I'm scared, that's all I can say. Something of his brain has been compromised."[11]

Open Head Injuries

Blows to the head like those sustained by Johnson and Mesi are serious, but the most severe brain injury occurs when a foreign object—a bullet, shrapnel from a bomb, or debris from a construction site—pierces the skull and lodges in the brain, causing an open head injury. In such cases, the patient not only suffers damage to brain cells, nerve fibers, and blood vessels but also is at high risk of developing a brain infection. Exposure to bacteria or other contamination can lead to many kinds of infection, with complications that can potentially increase brain swelling, delay recovery, and worsen the damaging effects of the injury. For instance, if a skull fracture involves tearing of the meninges, a potentially fatal infection known as meningitis can develop. Says Michael Paul Mason, "Open head injuries are a frightening mess, literally. Whether the insult comes from a bullet, a baseball bat, or a high-speed collision, the result is always chaotic and distressing. The scalp is so vascular [contains so many blood vessels] that blood pours liberally from any laceration. When bone is cracked or penetrated, shards invariably get lodged in the brain."[12]

Scanning the Brain for Trauma

When patients are brought to the emergency room with open head TBI, doctors can usually quickly determine the extent of the injury, and take the necessary steps to stabilize the wound and prepare the injured person for surgery. In the case of a suspected closed head TBI, physicians may have to do some detective work to diagnose the trauma.

First, vital signs—blood pressure, pulse, body temperature, and ability to breathe—will be checked and stabilized. Next, the doctor will ask the patient a series of questions that could indicate impaired cognitive abilities: *What's your name? Where are you? What day is it?* The doctor may ask the patient to perform simple tasks, such as wiggling toes or holding up fingers. The doctor will ask the patient to open and close his or her eyes, move limbs, and speak.

While in the emergency room, the doctor may be able to make a quick assessment of the pressure on the brain by using an ophthalmoscope, an instrument that allows doctors to look at the back of the eyes for evidence that the brain is under pressure. After the initial examination in the emergency room, the doctor may order other tests and scans.

The doctor will likely order an X-ray screening of the patient's skull. X-raying an injury is one of the most routine of all

An ophthalmoscope is a useful tool in helping doctors determine whether the brain is under pressure.

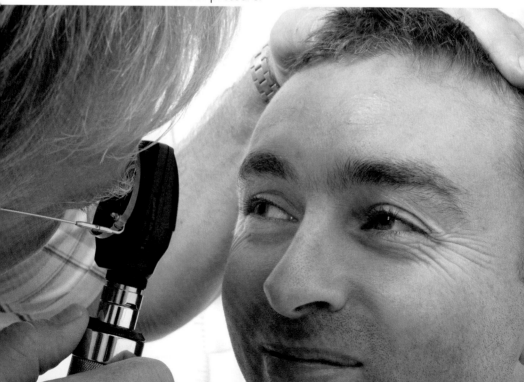

medical examinations, and physicians have used this technology for more than a century. X-ray scans are used to diagnose trauma to all bones, not just the skull. When shot through the human body, X-rays pass easily through soft objects such as skin and internal organs but are absorbed by bone and metal. In the hospital, the technician will record the X-rays on photographic film placed behind the traumatized body part. The whole process, from photographing to processing the film, can be accomplished in a few minutes.

X-rays are useful for detecting trauma to the skull but they do not give doctors a very clear picture of brain injuries—unless there is a foreign object such as a bullet or shard of glass lodged in the brain. However, whether or not the X-ray scan shows a skull fracture, if the doctor suspects that the brain has also sustained trauma, he or she will probably order additional examinations.

One of those is likely to be the computed tomography scan, or CT scan. The examination is also sometimes known as a computed axial tomography scan, or CAT scan. CT scans employ X-rays, but the screening is regarded as far more thorough than a simple X-ray image. A basic X-ray image gives the doctor a two-dimensional picture of the injury. During a CT scan, the patient lies inside a doughnut-shaped machine that employs special photographic equipment to encircle the body. As the X-rays enter the body from all angles, different tissues absorb different amounts of X-ray radiation. The CT scanner measures the radiation, converting it into electrical impulses. A computer then uses the electrical impulses to create a three-dimensional image of the injury that is displayed on a monitor. According to the American Association of Neurological Surgeons:

> A computed tomography scan (CT or CAT scan) is the gold standard for the radiological assessment of a TBI patient. A CT scan is easy to perform and is an excellent test for detecting the presence of blood and fractures, which are the most crucial [injuries] to identify in medical trauma cases. Plain X-rays of the skull are recommended

by some as a way to evaluate patients with only mild neurological dysfunction. However, most centers in the United States have readily available CT scanning, which is a more accurate test.[13]

Another technology that is often employed to detect brain trauma is magnetic resonance imaging, or MRI. As with a CT scan, the MRI patient lies on a table inside a machine shaped like a doughnut. The MRI doughnut is actually a huge magnet that energizes certain atoms in human cells. During the screening procedure, the scanner broadcasts radio waves through the body that strike the energized cells and are translated into an image. An MRI scan can reveal far more about soft tissue than either an X-ray or CT scan can; therefore, MRI is regarded as a very valuable tool for detecting brain trauma. A drawback of the MRI scan is that it may take up to an hour or more to produce a series of images—much longer than X-rays or CT scans, which is why MRI scans are not typically used in emergency situations.

Another diagnostic test that is often used in nonemergency situations is the electroencephalogram, or EEG. The purpose of the EEG is to detect the amount of electrical activity in the brain, which drives the impulses transmitted by the axons and dendrites. In preparation for an EEG, up to twenty-five adhesive metal disks are placed on the patient's skull. These disks are electrodes, which are connected by wires to the EEG machine. The electrodes transmit the electrical activity in the brain into the EEG machine, which displays the brain's activity in the form of wavy lines that appear on a monitor. If brain trauma exists, the EEG may be able to pick up the region of the brain where the electrical activity has been interrupted by the injury. It can take two hours or more to perform an EEG test, which is why doctors may not order an EEG if the patient is in need of immediate treatment.

Before the development of CT and MRI technology in the 1970s, physicians often relied on angiograms to detect trauma to blood vessels inside the brain. When an angiogram is per-

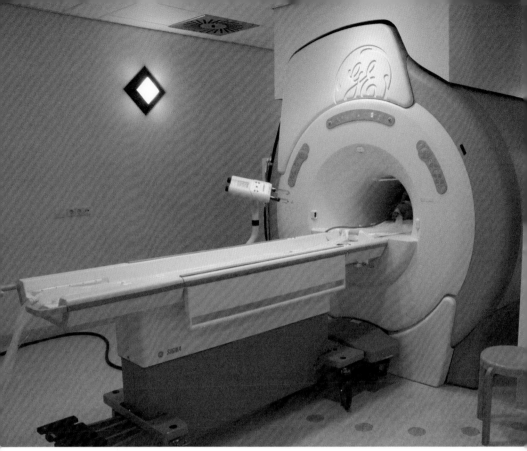

An MRI machine is often used to detect brain trauma.

formed, a dye is first injected into the patient's bloodstream. X-rays are then shot through the traumatized region of the head to detect leaks in blood vessels, which are highlighted by the dye. CT and MRI scans do a very good job of detecting trauma to blood vessels in the brain. However, angiograms may still be employed by the doctor to detect a tear, which is known as a dissection, in the carotid artery, which is located in the neck and supplies blood to the brain. A tear in the carotid artery can lead to a stroke.

If brain swelling is a concern, the doctor may order intra-cranial pressure, or ICP, monitoring. During ICP monitoring, a plastic tube is inserted into the brain through the skull via a hole drilled by a surgeon. The tube senses the pressure inside the skull and transmits measurements to a recording device. If necessary, the tube can also be used to draw out fluid and relieve pressure on brain tissue. This form of monitoring is usually reserved for critical trauma cases; typically, the patient is already unconscious when the physician makes the decision to drill through the skull.

Profound Impacts

Medical science has done a very good job of finding ways to detect TBI. If the trauma is mild, such as a concussion, chances are the condition will clear up on its own without further complications. Other cases, which may involve bleeding in the brain or trauma that results in open head wounds, are obviously far more serious and can have devastating consequences, such as amnesia, stroke, and cognitive impairments.

CHAPTER TWO

How Do Brains Get Traumatized?

Traumatic brain injuries can occur anywhere at any time but at least one in five occur on football fields, in boxing rings, on hockey rinks, and in similar places where contact sports, both amateur and professional, are played. Professional athletes may have access to the best protective gear, sports medicine specialists, and treatments available and still sustain brain trauma. The case of Eric Lindros provides an example of a highly skilled professional athlete whose career was cut short by TBI.

Lindros, an all-star center for the Philadelphia Flyers in the National Hockey League, sustained a head injury in a 2000 game. Elbowed in the head by an opposing player, Lindros collapsed to the ice. His regulation helmet had failed to provide his brain with adequate protection. Lindros was helped to the locker room, where he vomited. After the game, Lindros suffered from a severe headache and complained of seeing strange colors. The team doctor gave him ibuprofen, an over-the-counter pain medication, and cleared him to play in the team's next game. "I knew that things were not good, and I tried to convey that through my symptoms," Lindros said. "But I was not going to pull myself out of the game."[14]

Lindros's symptoms persisted. Nine days after the injury, Lindros finally saw a specialist in brain trauma who diagnosed a moderate concussion. The doctor told Lindros that if he sustained a second concussion before the first trauma healed, the result could be permanent brain damage. Lindros sat out the next ten weeks of the season but soon after returning to the team sustained another concussion. This time, doctors advised him to retire. Lindros refused and continued playing until 2007, when he finally left the sport. In the meantime, he sustained several more concussions and never again achieved the superstar status that he had enjoyed prior to the 2000 season. "I wanted to keep playing," Lindros said. "That's the mentality of a player—'Everything's going to be fine, it's going to go away' and you just keep on playing."[15]

Traumatic brain injuries often occur in professional sports. Hockey player Eric Lindros sustained a head injury in a 2000 game and numerous other concussions until his retirement in 2007.

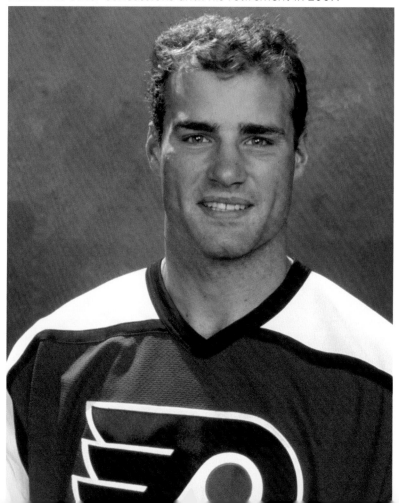

What Is Shaken Baby Syndrome?

Infants are very susceptible to traumatic brain injury. Their heads are the largest parts of their bodies and their necks aren't yet strong enough to support the weight and movements of their heads. When they are shaken, their heads can whip back and forth violently, causing concussion, ruptured blood vessels, brain swelling, and formation of blood clots. Also, they can sustain eye damage that can lead to blindness—a whiplash motion can result in detached retinas or scarring of their optic nerves.

Today such injuries are known as Shaken Baby Syndrome, or SBS. Typically, a baby is hurt by a parent, babysitter, or other caregiver who is angered by a fussing baby and shakes the infant in a tragically misguided effort to make the baby stop crying. "In other cases," adds pediatric nurse Celeste Wright, "SBS occurs from an accident. That is, the caregiver or parent might have simply been playing too roughly with the baby, throwing them in the air, holding them upside down, swinging them around, or jumping up and down with them."

Regardless of the circumstances, Shaken Baby Syndrome can be devastating to the child. A study performed in Canada looked at SBS patients ten years after their diagnoses and found that only 7 percent of the patients were leading normal lives. Twelve percent were still in comas or other vegetative states, 60 percent were living with some degree of mental disability, and 85 percent were found to be in need of ongoing care for the rest of their lives.

Quoted in Kristi Patrice Carter, "Shaken Baby Syndrome," *Pediatrics for Parents*, October 2001, p. 9.

Of course, playing sports is only one way in which people can sustain brain trauma. Accidents at home and in automobiles carry a risk of brain trauma. Riders who fall off their bicycles, even if they do wear helmets, can harm their brains. Victims of violent crime also often sustain brain trauma. Soldiers in combat zones are obviously at high risk of injuries of all kinds; in recent years, military personnel serving in Iraq and Afghanistan have been vulnerable to brain trauma from so-called improvised explosive devices, or IEDs. Insurgents in the two wars conceal and detonate these crude explosive devices, which are capable of spraying shrapnel over a wide area and penetrating helmets and armor.

Contact Sports

Lindros is among a long list of professional athletes who have seen their careers affected by TBI. Lindros's brother, Brett, also had to retire from professional hockey after sustaining a concussion. "My brother came back too soon," says Eric Lindros. "It wasn't even a head shot. It was a shot to the chest, shaking his skull. He was in bad shape. For the longest time, he couldn't even dial a phone. He'd have a phone with these huge numbers on it."[16]

Shortly after retiring from professional hockey, Eric Lindros was named ombudsman for the National Hockey League (NHL) Players Association, the union that represents NHL players. As ombudsman Lindros serves as an advocate for players' rights, particularly in health-related matters. Since accepting the job, Lindros has pressed the NHL for additional monitoring of players who have suffered brain trauma to ensure that they are not permitted to take the ice before their injuries have fully healed. He has also called for referees to be more vigilant in penalizing and ejecting players who deliver unfair and vicious blows to the heads of other players, which Lindros claims is on the rise. "The game has changed and the respect level has truly changed in what I've seen in the last seven years," says Lindros. "There's an unwritten code of conduct being stomped on and walked over. I don't ever recall seeing so many questionable hits as now."[17]

High-profile veterans such as Lindros have raised awareness of brain injury in professional sports. Athletes at other levels are not as fortunate. Even though the action may be slower and the hits not as hard, head injuries are still very common in college, high school, and community league sports, where they may go unreported and where the risk may be less well recognized.

Rick DiBlasi Jr., age thirteen, played in a spring hockey league in Buffalo, New York. During a game, he was sent sprawling by a hard check from an opposing player. After sustaining the hit, DiBlasi got to his feet, skated to the bench, and told his coach he felt fine. After resting for a few minutes, he skated back into the game.

After the game, though, DiBlasi complained of a headache. His parents gave him a Tylenol to ease the pain. Later DiBlasi went to a friend's house, where he played street hockey. After the game, he started vomiting. His friend's parents called an ambulance. At the hospital, DiBlasi was diagnosed with a concussion—which came as something of a relief to his parents, who thought his injury could have been much worse. "I started panicking," said DiBlasi's father, Rick DiBlasi Sr. "It was hours later, and I'm thinking it's something like a blood clot."[18]

DiBlasi may have avoided a much more severe head injury such as a blood clot because helmets, which can provide at least minimal protection, are standard equipment in ice hockey leagues. But helmets are not worn in all sports, and sometimes the lack of protection can prove unhealthy.

Athletes at all levels are at risk for head injuries.

As a high school freshman in Buffalo, Jessica Montmarquet earned a starting position on the varsity field hockey team. Generally, field hockey players do not wear helmets, though the action during a field hockey game can be quite physical. During a preseason practice, Montmarquet collided with another player and sustained a concussion. Suffering from severe headaches, dizziness, and nausea, she was forced to miss three weeks of the season. Her headaches continued after she returned to the lineup. At first her parents told her to tough it out. "Nobody wants their kids to be wimpy," said Montmarquet's mother, Kathy Montmarquet. "We told Jess that headaches are going to happen and you either sit out or play through it." Weeks passed, though, and Montmarquet's headaches persisted. During a game, she was jostled and felt the pain in her head intensify; she also felt dizzy and nauseated. After the game, Montmarquet underwent a CT scan, which showed no further brain damage but confirmed she suffered a concussion. This time, Montmarquet was benched until her headaches went away. "If I knew what I know now, I wouldn't have let her play [so soon]," said Kathy Montmarquet. "I guess, for us at least, initially you hear about concussions but you don't think about it being as serious as it is until in her case it continues as long as it did. It took me awhile to grasp the seriousness of it and what could ultimately happen."[19]

Heading the Ball

The incidence of concussions and other TBI is well known in contact sports such as ice hockey and field hockey. It is less well known that they are also common in games not regarded as contact sports, such as soccer. Justin Rutland, a thirteen-year-old boy from West Chester, Pennsylvania, died of brain trauma during a soccer match. After heading the ball, Justin returned to the sidelines where he complained of dizziness and a ringing in his ears. "He was sitting out and he fainted," said Justin's sister, Jiea Rutland-Simpson. "He never regained consciousness."[20] An autopsy determined that Justin had massive bleeding in his brain after heading the ball—an injury that

A young boy hits a soccer ball with his head. Studies show that heading the ball can cause brain trauma.

might have been avoided if Justin had worn headgear or if the technique of heading had been outlawed in youth soccer, as many advocates have demanded.

A 2000 study reported in the *Journal of Trauma, Injury, Infection, and Critical Care* found that the force of a soccer ball striking the head is 160 to 180 percent greater than the force of routine impacts sustained by football or ice hockey players who wear helmets. Said the author of the study, "It strikes me that any coach who permits or promotes heading a soccer ball by junior high school, high school, or college students puts not only the students at risk but is also personally at risk [for lawsuits]. Physicians involved with student athletes should take note of these findings and parents should also become concerned."[21]

Another study reported that concussions are quite common in soccer. A report prepared for the National Collegiate Athletic Association (NCAA), the governing body for most intercollegiate sports in America, found that concussions account for 11 percent of all injuries sustained in women's soccer as well as 7 percent of all injuries sustained in men's soccer.

Other evidence suggests that even mild blows to the head during soccer games may have a cumulative effect. A study performed by the Medical College of Virginia tested sixty soccer players who said they frequently head the ball, and found that their levels of concentration, attention span, and overall mental functioning were lower than those of soccer players who said they generally do not head the ball during matches. The *American Journal of Sports Medicine* reports, "The cumulative effects of repeated injuries, even mild injuries, over time remains a serious concern to those involved in sports medicine. The fact that some athletes do not recover as expected from concussions and are hampered by persistent symptoms for weeks or months is troublesome."[22]

Weekend Chores

While brain trauma is always a concern on the athletic field, at least many athletes do take precautions. Helmets are common in contact sports such as football, ice hockey, and lacrosse. Baseball and softball players typically wear helmets when they bat and run the bases. Even youth T-ball leagues require their very young players to wear helmets. Participants in equestrian events wear helmets as they compete on horseback. Amateur boxers also wear padded headgear that provides them with some protection against blows to the head. Race car drivers wear helmets as well.

But head injuries outside of the sports arena usually occur when people are not wearing head protection. People involved in car accidents and people who slip on icy sidewalks or in their bathtubs cannot rely on even the modest protection that helmets provide. It is true that many construction workers, heavy machinery operators, and other laborers wear protective headgear on the job, but it isn't likely that a homeowner undertaking a weekend fix-up chore dons a helmet before climbing a ladder.

Robert Anderson, the superintendent of the Jamesville–
DeWitt School District near Syracuse, New York, had been
spending the Labor Day weekend in 1995 painting the second-
story trim of his house when he fell off a ladder and struck his
head on his concrete driveway. "I had just painted that part of
the house the day before," Anderson said later. "Why I fell, I
don't know. I'll never know. No one saw it. My son was home,
and he came out and found me on the ground."[23]

Anderson was unconscious when his son found him sprawled
on the driveway. The school superintendent spent the next five

Falls from ladders frequently result in head injuries since people
rarely wear helmets while working around the house.

days in a coma. After regaining consciousness, Anderson was forced to undergo months of physical and mental therapy before he was able to return to his job.

Working atop a ladder is the type of risky activity that can result in TBI as well as broken bones. According to the U.S. Consumer Product Safety Commission, each year more than 160,000 Americans injure themselves in falls from ladders. Of course, people tend to do other risky things that often result in head injuries. Andrew Klein, sixteen, suffered a fractured skull after the driver of an all-terrain vehicle lost control, catapulting Andrew, a passenger, headfirst into a rocky ridge. Klein spent a week in a coma. When he emerged from the coma, the

Common Causes of TBI

Falls are the most common mishaps that cause traumatic brain injury, according to the U.S. Centers for Disease Control and Prevention (CDC), which reported in 2006 that 28 percent of all TBI occur when people fall and strike their heads. The second most common cause of TBI is motor vehicle accidents, which the CDC said accounts for 20 percent of head injuries in America.

Another common cause of TBI is what the CDC calls "struck by/against events," which account for 19 percent of head injury cases. This category includes people who are struck by cars or other moving objects, such as baseballs, debris that might fly about a construction site, or an elbow swung by an opposing hockey player. It also includes injuries sustained by people who walk into objects, such as glass doors they thought were open. Violent crime also accounts for a large share of head injuries. The CDC reports that 11 percent of TBI is caused by assaults.

Other causes of TBI include accidents involving motorcycles and bicycles, which account for 3 percent of brain injuries; mishaps that occur on other forms of transportation, such as trains, buses and airplanes (2 percent); and suicide attempts (1 percent). The CDC reports that 7 percent of TBI is caused by various other factors, and the cause of 9 percent of head injury cases is unknown.

teen's first words were, "I'm dying."[24] Though he had regained consciousness, Klein did not recognize his parents. He eventually recovered his memory; he left the hospital and graduated from high school as an honors student. Still, for the rest of his life, he will carry a metal plate in his head, inserted to repair the gash in his skull.

The fact that Klein, a teenage boy, was riding in an all-terrain vehicle without a helmet illustrates an important TBI statistic—teenage boys and young men are more likely than other population groups to engage in risky behavior, and therefore are more likely than others to sustain head injuries. According to the U.S. Centers for Disease Control and Prevention (CDC), each year more than eight hundred thousand people under the age of twenty-five suffer brain trauma, with the age group of fifteen- to nineteen-year-olds most at risk. In this age group, the CDC reports, one in about ten thousand young people are likely to sustain brain trauma and 17 percent of those cases will be fatal. The CDC further reports, that boys are 1.5 times more likely than girls to suffer head injuries.

Other Unanticipated Risks

Most people do not regard the act of riding in a car as risky behavior, but there is certainly a dangerous element to driving—particularly in inclement weather. Melissa Felteau of Ottowa, Canada, was injured in a car accident when the vehicle in which she was riding struck another car head-on during a snowstorm. In addition to serious internal injuries, she suffered significant trauma to the parts of the brain that control vision and other sensory organs as well as cognitive abilities. After her release from the hospital, Felteau, the director of public relations at a psychiatric hospital, developed a stutter, found it difficult to concentrate—she felt as though she was always under sedation—and experienced problems with her vision and memory

Before the accident, she was a gifted athlete and a competitive swimmer, skier, and whitewater kayaker. Her TBI affected her physical coordination, however. After the accident she

Car crashes are a significant cause of head injuries.

often fumbled coffee mugs, pencils, and books and found it difficult to keep her balance when she walked. Persistent amnesia has been a problem too. "Names are very important to me," Felteau says. "You can imagine how embarrassing it was for me to be the public relations director and not remember names."[25]

Famous people too have been known to risk head injuries that put their very lucrative careers in jeopardy. In 2006, for example, Rolling Stones guitarist Keith Richards was vacationing on Fiji in the South Pacific when he shinnied up a palm tree to pick coconuts. On the way down, Richards slipped and fell, banging his head on the hard surface below. Richards suffered a concussion. "Picking coconuts is quite common on the island," a local resident told a newspaper reporter. "It's just that Keith had a bit of an accident coming down."[26]

The mishaps that caused the brain trauma suffered by Anderson, Klein, Felteau, and Richards show how head injuries can occur when people are doing things most people would regard as quite ordinary. The consequences, however, can be catastrophic; according to CDC statistics, some fifty thousand Americans die each year from traumatic brain injuries.

Wounded in War

By 2008 America's wars in Afghanistan and Iraq had cost the lives of nearly five thousand members of the American military and wounded another thirty thousand soldiers. TBI has become the most common injury among military personnel wounded in these conflicts. Recent studies by physicians at Walter Reed Army Medical Center in Washington, D.C., which treats most of the wounded, found TBI in at least 60 percent of the injured veterans who have returned from the two wars.

Improvements in battlefield medicine and body armor have saved the lives of many wounded soldiers and marines who otherwise would have died from their injuries. However, many of those who now survive even horrific wounds are returning to America to face a lifetime of debilitating brain trauma. "They're surviving where they wouldn't have survived before," says Tim Silver, chief of physical medicine at Hunter Holmes McGuire Veterans Administration Medical Center in Virginia. "But they're walking away with lasting effects of the head injury."[27]

John Sims, a fifty-one-year-old Army National Guard warrant officer, nearly died when his Black Hawk helicopter crashed in Iraq in 2003. He sustained brain trauma in the crash and, after returning to America, could no longer perform his job as a commercial airline pilot. He suffered from severe amnesia and could not even recognize people who are closest to him, including his wife, Violeta. "Six months after the injury, he received amnesia and forgot who I was," Violeta Sims said. "This is a person with the same body, but he's different, very different."[28]

Army National Guard major Russ Smith sustained a much milder injury in Iraq—he was struck by debris from a missile fired at the U.S. embassy in Baghdad. He was diagnosed with mild TBI; nevertheless, the injury has affected his life. Smith was knocked unconscious by the blast; he lost some of his hearing and suffers from chronic headaches and memory loss. He has also noticed some differences in his personality. Smith says he is more short-tempered and impatient: "I try to be conscious of my moods because I know I'm irritable."[29]

The Ultimate Cost

Of course, many members of the military pay the ultimate cost, losing their lives in battle. In 2006 *National Geographic* reporter Neil Shea accompanied army medic David Mitchell and other medical responders into the field in Iraq to report on their fight to save the lives of wounded soldiers. In one case, Mitchell's team worked feverishly to save a soldier who suffered a chest wound. During a frantic few minutes, Mitchell and the other medics applied what they believed were lifesaving measures to seal the man's wounds, stop the bleeding, and help him to start breathing again. After stabilizing the wound, Mitchell's team turned him over to army doctors, believing they had saved the soldier's life. Sadly, the doctors discovered a piece of shrapnel had penetrated the man's brain—it was embedded too

Traumatic brain injury is the most common injury among military personnel stationed in Iraq and Afghanistan.

deeply to remove through surgery, and within minutes the head wound proved fatal. As Shea reported:

> They pumped in pain meds, just in case and waited for his heart to stop. For Mitchell, the flare of triumph dies. He looks at me blankly, then walks away, saying nothing. It doesn't always end like this. But these are the days the crews must get used to, the ones they never forget.[30]

Brain injury can happen to anyone—among the people who have suffered concussions and other head trauma are professional athletes like Eric Lindros, teenagers like Jessica Montmarquet and Rick DiBlasi Jr., rock stars like Keith Richards, soldiers like Russ Smith, and homeowners like Robert Anderson. All have something in common: One moment they are going about their lives—skating in an NHL game, enjoying a vacation on a South Seas island, painting the house, or walking point on a surveillance mission in Baghdad—and the next they have suffered a blow to the head, sustaining injuries that could forever change their lives.

CHAPTER THREE

Living with Brain Trauma

Most of the 1.5 million Americans who sustain head injuries each year recover in a brief time and do not suffer long-term effects. Still, according to the CDC, some ninety thousand people a year who sustain brain trauma will suffer long-term, possibly life-long, disabilities.

Many of them will develop symptoms of dementia—a progressive decline in their ability to think, solve problems, communicate, and recall information. Dementia is closely linked to Alzheimer's disease, a fatal brain disorder mostly associated with increasing age (sixty-five and older). Many advanced-stage Alzheimer's patients require round-the-clock care in nursing facilities because eventually their basic cognitive functions are lost—they cannot recall their own names or recognize the faces of loved ones, and in many cases can no longer use utensils to eat, brush their teeth, use the toilet, or bathe themselves.

Researchers now believe serious head injury increases a person's risk of developing Alzheimer's disease. Indeed, many brain trauma patients start exhibiting similar symptoms at a much younger age than the average onset of Alzheimer's. As they spiral into the fog of dementia, routine daily activities become more and more of a challenge. Simple tasks will eventually become very difficult. Their lives and the lives of their family members, who must take care of them, will change forever. A report by the CDC summarizes the impact of serious impairment caused by early-onset Alzheimer's or by traumatic damage to the regions of the brain responsible for cognitive function:

> A traumatic brain injury may permanently alter a person's career or vocational aspirations and may also have profound effects on social and family relationships. In part, impairment of cognitive function may result in loss of communication skills and memory, inability to organize tasks and solve problems, and decreased attention to detail. TBI may also cause emotional instability—especially impulsiveness—and changes in the ability to see, smell, and hear.[31]

Not all TBI patients develop dementia. Many develop other symptoms that are less serious than dementia, such as migraine headaches and insomnia, but even subtle or more manageable symptoms can have a profound effect on a person's life if the condition is chronic or the impairment is progressive. Some patients experience psychological changes: the onset of depression or a change in personality, a tendency to be short-tempered or overemotional, reacting to minor problems with fits of anger or sobbing. The most extreme cases are represented by patients whose brain function is so impaired that they have lapsed into permanent comas or similar vegetative states—unable to see, hear, or respond to others. Some patients exist in these states indefinitely; others stay alive only with the help of ventilators or other artificial life support.

Punch Drunk

Two of the most well known examples of the effects of brain trauma are Muhammad Ali and Jerry Quarry. Both famed boxers enjoyed long and illustrious careers but both have suffered from long-term consequences of brain atrophy—wasting away of brain tissue—caused by the repeated poundings they took in the ring.

Quarry was a tough, rawboned scrapper who boxed professionally for eighteen years, compiling a 53–9–4 record. Looking back over his career, some experts speculate that he spent too long in the ring. Even before he retired from boxing, Quarry was already displaying symptoms of dementia. But he kept boxing, finally retiring after a knockout in 1983. Quarry returned to the ring once more in 1992 at the age of forty-seven—in which he took a brutal pounding over six rounds at the hands of cruiserweight Ron Cramner, sixteen years younger than Quarry.

Boxer Jerry Quarry suffered from long-term consequences of brain atrophy due to repeated poundings in the ring.

In 1995 Quarry was inducted into the World Boxing Hall of Fame. By then he was so disabled that he could not remember his name to sign autographs. Linda Rogers, director of the Southwest Institute for Clinical Research in California, where Quarry was a patient, remarked, "Jerry doesn't know where he's at or what month or day it is. When you ask him, his response is, 'It's not important to me.' He can't recall three items three minutes later."[32] His brother James added, "He hallucinates, he hears voices. When he walks off, we have to go find him. Sometimes, we can't find him, and we have to call the police and they bring him back."[33]

Quarry died in 1999 at the age of fifty-three. His brain trauma eventually led to organ failure. Doctors said the cause of death was dementia pugilistica—brain damage by repeated blows to the head, commonly called punch-drunk syndrome. Boxing was first linked with brain damage in 1928 when physician Harrison S. Martland published a paper in the *Journal of the American Medical Association* comparing the physical symptoms of former fighters to those of intoxicated individuals. Martland referred to the former fighters as "punch drunk" and found that they had trouble walking and suffered from short attention spans, poor memories, and slurred speech. In 2007 Stanley M. Aronson, the former dean of Brown University Medical School in Rhode Island, stated:

> The image of the "punch drunk," "slap happy," "slug nutty" former boxer entered the mainstream of motion pictures as a type of comic relief. Such cinematic characters were portrayed as fundamentally happy and carefree. Martland's remorseless data, however, showed that this syndrome was proportional to the number of bouts engaged in by the victim. The more the number of bouts, the greater the likelihood of enduring brain injury.[34]

Of course, there was nothing carefree about the Quarry case. Throughout the former boxer's ordeal, the Quarry family bore the burden of Jerry's care. Sadly, the family's burden became even heavier—Jerry's younger brother Mike was also a professional boxer and, like Jerry, also suffered from dementia pugilistica. He died in 2006 at the age of fifty-five, spending the final years of his life in nursing homes. About three months before his death, he lost the ability to walk and talk. "His brain was atrophying in many areas,"[35] said Robert Pearson, Mike Quarry's brother-in-law.

Parkinsonism and Muhammad Ali

During his career Jerry Quarry fought Muhammad Ali twice, losing both times. Indeed, Quarry was among a long list of boxers who challenged Ali during the 1960s and 1970s, only to lose to the fighter who called himself "the Greatest." Many boxing experts agree that Ali is the greatest heavyweight in the history of the sport. He rose to fame in 1960 when he won a gold medal at the Olympic Games in Rome, Italy. Soon after the Olympics, Ali turned pro and went on to compile a 56–5 record during a twenty-one-year career that made him one of the most recognizable people in the world.

Boxing experts and medical professionals alike also agree that Ali, like Quarry, spent too many years in the ring. In one of his last bouts, fought at the age of thirty-seven, he took a vicious pounding from heavyweight champion Larry Holmes. The fight was so one-sided that Holmes begged the referee to stop the bout. As legendary sportscaster Howard Cosell described the fight:

> Ali had convinced a lot of people that he could really whip Larry Holmes and win the heavyweight title for the fourth time. I wasn't one of them, and I told Ali so. There was no way Ali was going to beat Holmes, and he was a fool for trying. His speech was already slurred from the beatings he had taken through the years. He walked awkwardly. His hands seemed unsteady, and there was often a vacant look in his eyes. . . .
>
> It's hard to describe the terrible feelings I had covering that fight, watching Holmes reduce Ali to rubble. He was

the Greatest, and what an awful thing it was to watch him slumped and battered in a humiliating defeat.

Thinking back on it now, I am certain Ali's fight with Holmes exacerbated Ali's physical problems. In the years that followed, whenever we chanced to meet, it was practically impossible to carry on a cogent conversation with him.[36]

Indeed, soon after the Holmes fight Ali started displaying symptoms of parkinsonism—a syndrome similar to Parkinson's disease that includes slowed and slurred speech, muscle tremors, and rigid muscles—the result of the brain trauma he suffered in the ring. The syndrome is somewhat different than dementia pugilistica. In Quarry's case, the repeated blows to the head likely caused numerous concussions as well as actual shrinkage of the brain. Furthermore, Quarry's dementia and Alzheimer's-like symptoms were caused by a buildup of a chemical, beta-amyloid, in his brain. In Alzheimer's patients, the chemical acts like a sticky plaque that covers the brain

Muhammad Ali attends a congressional hearing on funding for a cure for Parkinson's disease in his role as spokesperson for the National Parkinson Foundation in 1998. Ali's Parkinson's symptoms are believed to have been caused by repeated blows to his head during his boxing career.

cells, prohibiting the neurons from transmitting messages to one another.

In Ali's case, the repeated blows to his head are believed to have diminished the number of cells in his brain that produce dopamine, the chemical that carries messages from cell to cell. Neurological research has shown that the brain contains many more neurons than it actually needs—it is nature's way of preserving cognitive abilities as people grow older and lose brain cells during the normal process of aging. In Parkinson's disease, the cells die much quicker, which means less dopamine is produced by the brain, leaving relatively young people fewer neurons than they need to maintain normal cognitive abilities. Ali's symptoms did not evolve through Parkinson's disease, but since the symptoms are similar he is said to suffer from parkinsonism.

One of the reasons Ali boasted of being the greatest of all time is that he was never knocked out in the ring. With skill, speed, savvy, and luck he managed to avoid the type of blow that could render him unconscious. But he absorbed many lesser punches that, on a cumulative basis, may have been more devastating than a single knockout punch. "Repetitive subconcussive blows are more damaging in the long run than occasional knockout blows,"[37] wrote the authors of a 1984 study linking parkinsonism to boxing.

Ali lives quietly at his home in Scottsdale, Arizona. He takes a variety of medications to help control his parkinsonism symptoms. He still receives fan mail and answers many of the letters, painstakingly signing autographs with trembling hands. His speech is so slurred that he is incapable of communicating with others. Family members say he spends his days watching videos of his fights. His wife Lonnie Ali says, "People are naturally going to be sad to see the effects of his disease, but if they could see him in the calm of his everyday life, they would not be sorry for him. He's at complete peace."[38]

Depression and Rage

As the cases of boxers Muhammad Ali and the Quarry brothers show, repeated blows to the head can have a variety of devastating effects on the brain and lead to a dramatic decline in the quality of life. The high-profile stories of athletes in other contact sports have drawn attention to other debilitating consequences of traumatic brain injury. Though he was not a boxer, former Pittsburgh Steelers lineman Mike Webster was also diagnosed with dementia pugilistica. During a sixteen-year career Webster played on four Super Bowl championship teams; when he was inducted into the Pro Football Hall of Fame in 1997 he was already showing signs of dementia, including memory loss and short attention span.

Since his retirement from the NFL in 1990, Webster had been unable to hold a job and was occasionally homeless, sleeping in his car or in bus stations. He was also showing signs of clinical depression, characterized by feelings of sadness, hopelessness, and inadequacy. People who suffer from depression often can't summon the energy to rise from their beds. In 1999 Webster was charged with forging a prescription to obtain an antidepressant

Brain trauma may have played a role in the murder/suicide case involving Canadian professional wrestler Chris Benoit in 2007. Doctors discovered that his brain was severely damaged, which could have led to his violent behavior.

drug. Finally his son Garrett took him in; by then, Webster was so troubled by depression that he often couldn't lift himself off the couch. "He has some brain injuries from football," Garrett Webster said. "I have to take care of my dad."[39] Mike Webster died in 2002 at the age of fifty. The cause of death was listed as a heart attack but the ex-player's death certificate also noted that he suffered from "chronic concussive brain injury."[40]

Brain trauma may also have played a role in the violence involving popular Canadian professional wrestler Chris Benoit in 2007. Born in Montreal in 1967, Benoit rose to Extreme Championship Wrestling stardom as the Canadian Crippler. His signature move was the diving head-butt: To finish off his opponent, he would climb to the top of the ropes and launch himself headfirst from 10 feet (3m) or more into his hapless adversary. He performed the stunt some two hundred times a year over the course of a twenty-two-year career.

In 2007 Benoit, his wife, and his seven-year-old son were found dead in their home; Benoit had murdered his family before taking his own life. Toxicology reports revealed a wide range of narcotics and performance-enhancing substances, such as steroids, in Benoit's body, which led many to charge that Benoit had gone on a murderous rampage as a result of steroid abuse. Doctors have long linked steroid abuse to a personality disorder called "roid rage," which provokes anger and violent hostility in the user.

But physicians who examined Benoit's brain tissue came to a different conclusion. Benoit's brain was severely damaged, doctors said, with similarities to the brains of other multiple-concussion athletes who harmed themselves or others. The doctors argued that Benoit's deadly violence could have been a consequence of the many concussions he suffered over the years. "We have always believed that people generally recover from concussions," says Bennet Omalu, the pathologist who examined Benoit's brain tissue, "but what we're finding is that some people may never really recover from recurrent concussions. . . . The damage is in your tissue."[41]

Writer Chris Nowinski, an advocate for athletes who have suffered brain trauma, looks at the effects of TBI on Mike Webster, the Quarry brothers, Muhammad Ali, and others and wonders whether he will suffer the same fate. Nowinski played football at Harvard University, then started a career as a professional wrestler. Along the way he sustained six concussions, forcing him to retire from wrestling after just three years in the business. As this is written, Nowinski's symptoms are not as severe as those suffered by other TBI patients, but he experiences migraine headaches, insomnia, mild depression, and occasional sleepwalking episodes. He thinks his symptoms may eventually become debilitating. "I have certain symptoms that are permanent and will probably get worse," Nowinski says. "Who knows how fast?"[42]

Personality Disorders

TBI can lead to mental illnesses. In addition to depression, TBI patients may also find themselves afflicted with personality disorders, mental illnesses that can change people from easygoing and friendly to suspicious, introverted, and unfriendly. Another former NFL star, Justin Strzelczyk, retired in 1998, evidently in perfect health. Within a few years, however, friends and family members started noticing a change in Strzelczyk's personality—formerly friendly and easygoing, he now seemed quick to anger. During conversations he became fixated on certain topics and would refuse to drop them. Moreover, his conversations became long and rambling, and he also confided to friends that he was having trouble sleeping and was hearing voices in his head. In addition, Strzelczyk harbored irrational fears, believing the government was spying on him.

In 2004 Strzelczyk got into his pickup truck and started driving. Hundreds of miles from home, he began speeding and driving erratically. Police chased Strzelczyk's truck for some 40 miles (64km) at speeds approaching 90 miles (145km) per hour. Finally the chase ended when Strzelczyk rammed his vehicle into a tanker truck. He was killed instantly. The autopsy on Strzelczyk's body reported evidence of dementia pugilistica.

Traumatic brain injuries may also lead to personality disorders. Football player Justin Strzelczyk's body showed evidence of dementia pugilistica, which manifested as a change in his personality.

In Strzelczyk's case, the symptoms manifested themselves in a dramatic change in the ex–football player's personality.

Army National Guard veteran Alec Gless also developed a personality disorder after he sustained a head wound in a truck crash in Iraq. At first Gless's injury didn't seem severe—an MRI scan did not reveal serious brain damage. Soon after returning to his home in Cannon Beach, Oregon, however, the formerly easygoing Gless became moody. Army doctors diagnosed Gless with post-traumatic stress disorder, an anxiety disorder prompted by memories of traumatic events that is a common ailment among veterans of warfare. But then Gless's memory started failing him—he bought a car and three days later forgot he made the purchase. After reexamining Gless the army doctors changed the diagnosis to TBI.

To make it through the day, Gless has to leave notes to himself around his home, reminding him what he needs to do. His social skills and ability to communicate with others also have degenerated and his moodiness persists. "It's like raising another kid," said Gless's wife, Shana. "We might think something like, 'That's an ugly shirt,' but we wouldn't say it. Alec would. It's almost like being with somebody who is drunk."[43]

Minimal Consciousness and Unconsciousness

As TBI patients like Gless struggle to overcome and adjust to their disabilities, other TBI patients are so severely injured by accidents, warfare, or strokes that they lack even the consciousness to begin the struggle. These saddest of all TBI cases include people who remain in comas as well as similar conditions doctors identify as a persistent vegetative state (PVS) or a minimally conscious state.

A coma is a deep state of unconsciousness. A comatose patient is alive but unable to move parts of his or her body or otherwise respond to others. Many coma patients require life support equipment such as ventilators to stay alive.

Patients in a persistent vegetative state exist on a level of consciousness just slightly above a coma. Patients experience wake and sleep cycles but have no awareness of what is going on around them. Steven Laureys, a coma researcher at the University of Liége in Belgium, states:

> These patients can usually breathe without technical assistance and can make a variety of spontaneous movements—such as grinding teeth, swallowing, crying, smiling, grasping another's hand, grunting or groaning—but these motions are always reflexive and not the result of purposeful behavior. Typically, patients will not fix their eyes on anything for a sustained period, but in rare instances they may briefly follow a moving object or turn fleetingly toward a loud sound.[44]

In many cases, the families of patients who remain in comas or persistent vegetative states must make end-of-life decisions for their loved ones. Many people prepare for the possibility that they will be unable to communicate their wishes directly

What Is Brain Dead?

The moment of death was historically understood to be the moment heartbeat and breathing stopped. Advances in medicine, however, make that definition problematic, because CPR (cardiopulmonary resuscitation) and defibrillation can sometimes restart a stopped heart, and life can sometimes be sustained by organ transplants or life-support devices even without a functioning heart or lungs. Today physicians and medical ethicists define biological death as "brain dead"—the moment electrical activity in the brain stops, irreversibly. The designation was established in 1968 by a Harvard Medical School committee trying to define irreversible coma. When life-support systems could maintain heart and lung function indefinitely, doctors needed a new legal definition of death that would enable them to declare a person dead and remove organs for transplant.

Several medical criteria must be met for a person to be declared brain dead. A physician will observe a patient's pupils to determine whether they still open and close in response to light; prod the patient with a needle or use other stimuli to determine whether the patient responds to pain; determine that the lungs can no longer draw breath without the help of a ventilator; and, finally, perform measurements of electrical activity in the brain through two EEG tests, which are administered at least twelve hours apart. Evidence of no electrical activity in the brain is generally accepted as the final confirmation that the patient is brain dead. At that point, doctors may harvest the patient's donated organs, which have been continuously supplied with oxygen by a ventilator, maximizing the chance for successful transplantation. Following the procedure to harvest the organs, the ventilator is removed from the body.

in case of a medical emergency—they draft documents known as living wills or advance directives in which they state what kind of treatment they do or don't want, and authorize another person to legally represent them in medical decisions. Many advance directives request family members to withhold or stop life-sustaining measures should an illness or accident leave the patient in a coma or PVS from which there is no chance of recovery. Such cases usually involve disconnecting a ventilator and allowing a patient who cannot breathe on his or her own to die, or disconnecting a feeding tube.

The most famous TBI case of this kind on record involved the fate of a Florida woman, Terri Schiavo, who remained in a PVS for fifteen years. In 1990 Schiavo suffered catastrophic brain damage when oxygen was cut off to her brain following a heart attack. She had no living will; diagnosed as being in a PVS, she spent most of the next fifteen years in skilled nursing facilities nourished by a feeding tube. In 2005 an appellate judge ruled that Schiavo's husband could authorize the removal of her feeding tube, after a long and bitter court battle with Schiavo's parents, who believed she still had a chance of recovering. An autopsy revealed substantial irreversible damage to all brain regions; nevertheless, the Schiavo case sparked controversy over the rights of PVS patients.

Patients who are diagnosed with minimal consciousness exist on a level just above the persistent vegetative state. In this condition, patients exhibit very minor signs of consciousness and awareness. They may be able to make the smallest of deliberate movements, such as a small verbal sound or motions with fingers. They can respond to language and can fix their eyes on the movement of objects and obey simple commands, but they cannot communicate with others.

This flyer was one of many posted by people urging action to prevent the removal of Terry Schiavo's feeding tube. The case sparked controversy over the rights of patients in a persistent vegetative state.

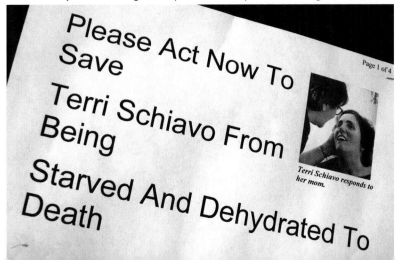

Please Act Now To Save Terri Schiavo From Being Starved And Dehydrated To Death

Page 1 of 4

Terri Schiavo responds to her mom.

The Right to Die

A document known as a living will or advance directive is a legally accepted way for a person to accept or decline medical treatment if he or she lapses into a coma or persistent vegetative state and cannot communicate directly with medical personnel. Many advance directives give family members permission to remove the patient from life support under certain conditions. When people make this type of advance arrangement, they are said to be exercising their right to die.

The right to die was established in a landmark 1976 case decided by the New Jersey Supreme Court in which the parents of Karen Ann Quinlan sought to remove their daughter from a ventilator after she spent a year in a coma. Quinlan had consumed drugs and alcohol at a party, which caused respiratory failure and irreversible brain damage. When it became clear to the Quinlans that their daughter would not recover, they asked the hospital to remove her from a ventilator. When the hospital refused, the Quinlans sued, claiming the medical center's decision violated their right to privacy. The court sided with the Quinlans and ordered the hospital to remove Karen Ann from life-sustaining equipment. After the patient was removed from the ventilator, she continued to breathe on her own and lived for another nine years. However, the case set a precedent that the rights of the individual had priority over medical professionals' duty to prolong life, clearing the way for family members to end or decline treatment and allow the death of patients who have no hope of recovery. Even though the courts have ruled in favor of the right to die, attorneys counsel people to write living wills and advance directives carefully and clearly to minimize confusion and conflict in such emotional situations.

The right to die was established in a case where Joseph and Julia Quinlan sought to remove their daughter, Karen Ann, from a ventilator after she spent a year in a coma.

Physicians have concluded that patients who have been in a coma or PVS for a year have no possibility of recovery. Patients who are in a minimally conscious state have a slightly better prognosis—a one-in-five chance of recovery. Although the odds are against them, patients have been known to recover from comas and similar conditions. In 2004, twenty-three-year-old Brian Sass suffered severe brain damage in a car accident. He spent a month in a coma. One day, at the end of her visit to his bedside, Sass's mother bent down to kiss his cheek. In the month since his accident, Sass had been unresponsive, but this time he emerged from his coma and kissed his mother back. "Did he kiss me?" Lorelei Sass asked her husband, Arthur. "Did you see that?" A moment later, Lorelei Sass said, "We both just started bawling our eyes out, because it was his way of saying, 'I'm in here.'"[45]

Heavy Toll

TBI takes a toll on patients and their families, but it also takes a financial toll on society. According to a CDC study, the costs of caring for TBI patients approach $38 billion a year. The CDC claims, "This study could not account for the intangible costs borne by families and friends of individuals who die prematurely from brain injury. For injured persons and their loved ones, the physical and emotional tolls from permanent disability are profound and impossible to quantify."[46]

Indeed, Muhammad Ali's family must constantly administer medications that help slow the deterioration of his cognitive abilities. Mike Webster's son cared for him during the final few months of his life. The Quarry family bore the responsibility of caring for Jerry and Mike as they descended further into dementia. The Gless family must endure Alec's mood swings and forgetfulness. Prior to serving in Iraq, Gless owned a business. Since sustaining TBI in the war, Gless has found that he can no longer handle the intellectual demands of his business. Now he works in a warehouse. He has often told his wife that a traumatic brain injury is the most difficult war wound to bear. Shana Gless remarks, "Alec says he would give us a limb to have his head back."[47]

CHAPTER FOUR

Treating and Preventing Brain Trauma

Although brain trauma can cause long-term disabilities, many people do eventually recover from their injuries and lead full lives. The brain has proven to be a very resilient organ, capable of repairing itself. Surgical techniques have also improved over the years, and thanks to the development of new, more precise surgical tools doctors are able to save healthy portions of the brain that otherwise would have been damaged during surgery.

What's more, rehabilitation therapists have made great strides in helping people recover from brain trauma. Today, with therapy, many brain-injured people can learn to talk again, walk again, and perform other functions they lost when their brains were injured. Indeed, doctors have found that even when large sections of the brain are cut away during surgery, the remaining parts can compensate by performing functions they did not previously perform. A part of the brain that was not used for communicating, for example, can learn to take over that function as the patient learns to talk again. Darryl Kaelin, director of the Acquired Brain Injury Program at Shepherd Center in Atlanta, Georgia, contends, "Early therapy helps brain cells that are bruised or stunned to recover their function faster. Later, rehab

56

trains brain cells not involved in a particular activity to pick up for the ones that have been destroyed."[48]

Still, for most patients it may take many months or even years to recover from traumatic brain injury. Although brain injuries often occur suddenly and without warning, experts agree that if TBI patients had taken some sensible precautions, many of them could have avoided the injuries that have placed their lives and mental health at risk.

Paramedics and Surgeons

The initial treatment of a TBI patient will probably be performed by paramedics or other so-called first responders. After arriving on the scene of an accident, a team of paramedics can help minimize damage to the brain by unblocking the patient's airway, providing breathing assistance, and keeping the blood circulating. If the brain continues to receive blood and oxygen, neurons can remain active and do not die during the aftermath of trauma. Quick response and competent emergency treatment is vital.

Surgeons perform brain surgery. Paramedics help to stabilize a TBI patient, but surgeons repair the damage.

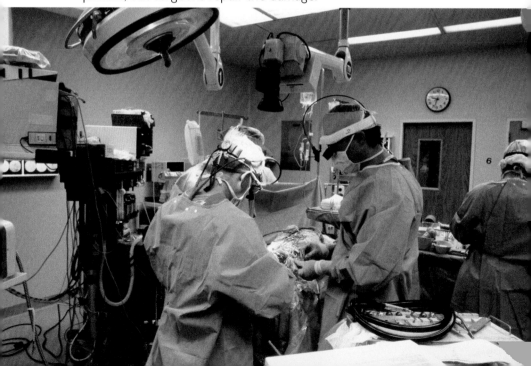

Paramedics may be able to stabilize the patient, but repairing the damage is the job of the surgeon. Doctors have been performing brain surgery for at least thirty-five hundred years. Evidence has surfaced describing brain surgery conducted by Egyptian physicians in the year 1550 B.C. In America today, about 2,850 physicians practice neurosurgery. In addition to responding to TBI, neurosurgeons also treat diseases of the brain, such as cancerous tumors, as well as diseases and trauma related to the spinal column.

The Smith Papyrus

Archaeologists have found evidence suggesting that Egyptian physicians practicing some thirty-five hundred years ago operated on the brains of their patients. Evidence also suggests the operations were not often successful.

An ancient scroll known as the Smith Papyrus—because it was unearthed in 1862 by an American archaeologist, Edwin Smith—includes a description of traumatic brain injury. Believed to have been written in 1550 B.C., the scroll provides advice to physicians on a number of injuries they might encounter. Regarding traumatic brain injury, the scroll advises,

> When you examine a man with a . . . wound on his head, which goes to the bone; his skull is broken. . . . Something is there . . . that quivers [and] flutters under your fingers like the weak spot in the head of a child which has not yet grown hard. The quivering and fluttering under your fingers comes because the brain of his skull is broken open. Blood flows from his two nostrils.

> Then you must say: a man with a gaping wound in his head; a sickness which cannot be treated.

Quoted in Jurgen Thorwald, *Science and Secrets of Early Medicine*. New York: Harcourt, Brace and World, 1962, p. 54.

In some cases, brain surgery is performed while the patient has been administered a local anesthetic, just enough to numb the scalp. This is possible because there are no pain receptors in the skull and brain. Surgeons often want the patient awake and alert during the operation so that he or she can follow instructions. During the surgery the doctor may ask the patient a series of questions or instruct the patient to wiggle his or her toes. By using the patient's responses as a guide, the doctor can avoid shaving away too much brain matter that may leave the patient debilitated after the surgery. Of course, in many severe TBI cases the patient arrives in the emergency room unconscious, leaving the surgeons no option other than to perform the operation without guidance from the patient.

Scalpels and Saws

Many operations on TBI patients are performed using knives, scalpels, saws, and other simple instruments. While visiting Balad Air Base in northern Iraq, Michael Paul Mason witnessed surgery performed by military physician Mark Melton on a young Iraqi boy, Jassim, who was injured in a bomb blast at a mosque. As Mason described the surgery,

> Melton runs a scalpel across and under the skin, then pulls a large piece of it off Jassim's head and lays it on the table near his ear. With the scalp cleared away, the underlying bone fracture is apparent. The glistening white skull looks cracked and cobbled at the very crown of the head. . . . Melton uses a small set of pliers to pry the bone fragments away. At moments, he has to wrench the cracked bone free. A pile of small skull chips collects near the discarded scalp.[49]

Other hospitals are equipped with far more advanced tools than Melton used in Iraq. For example, some surgeons can use ultrasound devices to blast away damaged brain tissue. The equipment, which employs sound waves, is mostly used to destroy cancerous tumors in the brain, but some surgeons have

Surgeons use a variety of scalpels and other tools during brain surgery.

found that it can be effective in cutting away brain tissue damaged during traumatic incidents. Modern drills that can actually liquefy brain matter have also been employed by surgeons. This technique is regarded as a less invasive method of clearing away damaged brain tissue than cutting it off with a scalpel.

Other doctors substitute Gamma Knife radiosurgery for scalpel surgery. This technique employs beams of gamma radiation to slice away damaged brain tissue. Hospitals in the United States have been slow to adopt Gamma Knife radiosurgery because the Gamma device is expensive; the apparatus costs $3.5 million plus another $500,000 to install. The patient who undergoes the surgery wears a helmet containing some two hundred small round holes. The gamma rays are then shot through the holes but aimed at the trouble spot so they can attack the damaged tissue from many angles. Using the Gamma Knife procedure, physicians can seal the leaks in damaged blood vessels in the brain.

Gamma Knife radiosurgery is regarded as an advance over surgery with a scalpel because the procedure does not require opening the skull—the gamma rays can be shot through bone.

Since the surgeons do not cut open the skulls of their patients, they rely heavily on MRI and CT scans to aim the gamma rays. The procedure is bloodless, which reduces the risk of complications and infections.

These surgical techniques have helped reduce the death rate for TBI while helping patients recover more quickly from their injuries. According to CDC statistics, the death rate for TBI has declined by 20 percent since 1980; meanwhile, the hospitalization rate for TBI patients has been reduced by 50 percent. In fact, hospital stays for some Gamma Knife radiosurgery patients have been cut by as much as 90 percent.

The Brain Heals Itself

Certainly, modern surgical techniques have a lot to do with why people are better able to recover from TBI, but the resilience of the brain is an important factor. Doctors as well as therapists have concluded that the brain contains an incredible ability to heal itself. Mason says:

> We tend to think of our brains as a coil of fixed connections, like a complicated electrical panel that reroutes messages back and forth. In recent years, neuroscience has revealed that the brain has a dynamic proclivity for self-recovery. In a global sense, the brain can actually relocate functions from one area of the brain to another. On a microscopic level, the neurons themselves can react to changes by making new connections. From a certain perspective, the brain acts like a switchboard that rewires itself when there's a short circuit. This sublime attribute, brain plasticity, yields wonder upon wonder.[50]

Though the brain is very good at repairing itself, it often takes several months or even years for new neurons to form or for other neurons to take over the functions of cells destroyed during the trauma. In 1984 Terry Wallis, then twenty years old, drove his truck through a guardrail and off a 25-foot (7.6m) rise near his home in Mountain View, Arkansas. The car tumbled down the hill. When emergency responders pulled Wallis from the wreckage he was unresponsive. He spent three months in a coma, then opened his eyes. Doctors upgraded his condition to a minimally conscious state, where he spent the next nineteen years unable to communicate with others.

In 2003 his mother visited the nursing home where Wallis lived. As she sat by his bedside, Wallis suddenly said, "Mom." Over the next few days, he added other words to his vocabulary. In fact, his second word was "Pepsi"—he had asked for the soft drink, his favorite. Since then, Wallis has taken additional steps toward recovery. He has moved out of the nursing home and now lives with his parents. He has also learned to

Terry Wallis demonstrated the regenerative powers of the brain after he awoke from a coma nineteen years after his 1984 car accident. His wife, Sandra, stands beside him.

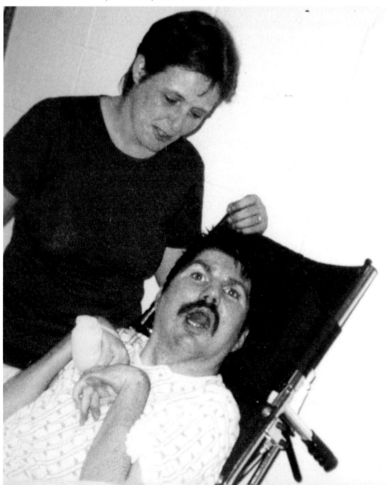

say many more words and count to twenty-five, but he is still confined to a wheelchair, needs help eating, and must receive nursing care. The effects of TBI are still evident—his attention span remains very brief.

Nonetheless, doctors have theorized that Wallis's brain repaired some of the damage on its own, using spare neurons to replace those damaged in the accident. Nicholas Schiff, a neurologist at Weill Cornell Medical School in New York, states, "In essence, Terry's brain may have been seeking new pathways to re-establish functional connections to areas involved in speech and motor control—to compensate for those lost to damage."[51]

The fact that Wallis is currently conscious and communicative has helped him regain more and more of his cognitive functions. Now therapists can work with Wallis, helping him learn new words and perform skills with his hands. In the years since he awoke from his minimally conscious state, Wallis has gone from being completely paralyzed from the neck down to regaining minimal movement in his hands and feet.

Learning Social Skills

For patients who are conscious and able to participate in their own recoveries, therapists prefer to start brain rehabilitation as soon after the trauma occurs as possible. Ideally, they want new neurons to begin functioning as soon as the cells develop. In most brain trauma cases, patients undergo speech and occupational therapies.

In speech therapy, patients learn how to talk again. It may be necessary for the therapist to teach the patient how to sound out simple words, much the way young children learn to pronounce words in elementary school. Words with multiple syllables will be broken into smaller pieces. The patient will be asked to repeat the pieces of each word over and over again. As the patient improves and learns new words, the therapist will teach the patient how to participate in a conversation by waiting his or her turn to respond, and how to carry on a conversation when there are many distractions, such as how to speak with others in a noisy restaurant.

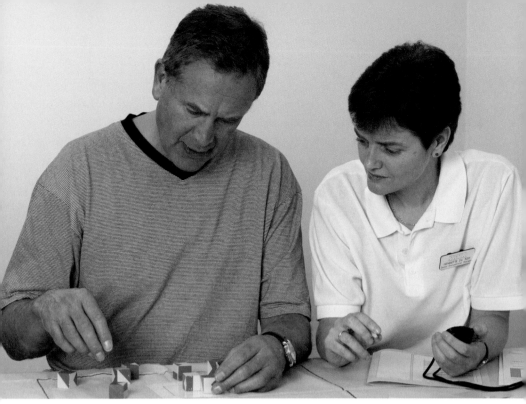

An occupational therapist works with her patient. Occupational therapy helps patients retrain their brains so they can return to a normal life.

Occupational therapy is designed to help the patient return to a normal life. After a traumatic brain injury, a patient may have forgotten how to get dressed, brush teeth, comb hair, and perform dozens of other tasks. At Kessler Institute for Rehabilitation in Saddle Brook, New Jersey, occupational therapist Jodi Levin works with about seven TBI patients at a time. One of her patients is an eighteen-year-old man who sustained brain trauma in a motorcycle accident. Remarkably, the man sustained no injuries to his body, but the brain trauma has affected his ability to function. He can't move his limbs because his brain does not send signals to his arms and legs.

Levin has designed a series of exercises to help the patient relearn the use of his limbs so that he can perform simple tasks for himself. In one exercise she kneels behind the patient and props him up using her arms. In front of the patient, the man's mother slowly passes photographs of family members by his face while Levin asks the patient to follow the photographs with his head. During the exercise, the man manages to crane his neck slightly from side to side. Levin regards that as an accomplishment. "I'm working on trunk control," she says. "It's the basis of everything—for getting out of bed, brushing teeth, getting dressed."[52]

Another brain trauma patient under Levin's care was involved in an automobile accident—his head slammed into the windshield. Doctors had to cut away a piece of his skull to reduce the swelling in his brain. The surgery has affected his motor control; he finds it very difficult to walk and use his hands. To help improve his motor skills, Levin taught him to swat at a balloon with a tennis racket. He also worked with a therapy dog, which led him on walks across a gym floor. The patient spent about a month at Kessler, then was able to return home, although he still returns to the center for outpatient therapy and so Levin can monitor his progress. "He's a miracle,"[53] says Levin.

The patients under Levin's care suffered brain trauma that left them severely debilitated, but even patients who received lesser degrees of TBI may also need therapy to help them return to normal lives. Iraq War veteran Jason Walsh sustained a head injury caused by a roadside bomb. At first, Walsh's brain injury seemed to be mild, but during his recovery at Walter Reed Hospital, Walsh noticed his personality changing—he was quick to anger, often lashing out at his parents and a brother during their visits. The personality change was likely caused by damage to Walsh's frontal lobes, the area of the brain that controls behavior. "Part of what you need your frontal lobes for is to figure out who you are, because you need that to plan your way of life," says Warren Lux, a Walter Reed neurosurgeon. "That means that people who have all the skills to do things in the world won't use them because they don't know who they are."[54]

Walsh also noticed his memory failing him. One morning he simply could not figure out how to put on a pair of sweatpants. After a period of recovery at Walter Reed, the army sent Walsh to a brain rehabilitation center in Virginia where he received therapy to help him train his memory and control his moods.

The Strange Case of Phineas Gage

The strange case of Phineas Gage proved the human brain's ability to withstand trauma as well as the crude surgical techniques of the nineteenth century. In 1847 Gage was severely injured while blasting rock to lay railroad tracks in Vermont. He was struck in the head by an iron bar that pierced his skull like an arrow. Miraculously he survived the accident as well as the operation to remove the iron bar, losing only the vision in his left eye, which had been pierced by the chunk of iron.

Gage's case also proves, however, that TBI can lead to mental illness and personality change. Prior to sustaining the injury, Gage was regarded as easygoing, energetic, and intelligent and was well liked by others. After his accident he became a man of little patience, quick to grow angry, cool to the opinions of others, unable to finish jobs, and foulmouthed. He died in 1860, thirteen years after the accident.

The physician who removed the rod, John Harlow, became something of a celebrity in the medical community, as he wrote about the surgery and lectured on the case for many years. As for the rod, Harlow donated it to Harvard Medical School's Warren Anatomical Museum in Boston, Massachusetts, where it remains on display.

His therapist has worked with Walsh to make up a grocery list, take it to the store, shop, and return home. Many people would take such light duties for granted, but for Walsh they have proven to be a challenge. By successfully carrying out a shopping errand, Walsh can learn how to plan his day, navigate through chores, and use his memory. For example, since he takes the bus to the grocery store, Walsh will have to remember where to find the bus stop, the coins he'll need for the fare, and where to get off the bus.

To help Walsh control his moods, the army has assigned him to an administrative job where he has the opportunity to interact with people and relearn social skills. For Walsh, the progress has been slow. "Sometimes I have to stop and think," he says. "It's pretty embarrassing. I'm aware that [my memory] is not back yet. I can feel myself think slower, step by step, instead of just reacting. I hate it."[55]

Exercising the Brain

Walsh hopes to one day return to active duty and become an instructor, perhaps even to return to a war zone. These duties would require a high level of cognitive ability. For Walsh and other TBI patients, such accomplishments are not out of the question. Indeed, it is not unusual for TBI patients to recover and go on to lead lives and careers that require a high level of cognitive ability.

As a twelve-year-old girl in Russia, Asya Schween struck a brick wall while riding her bicycle. She walked home, but that night she became very ill. She vomited in her bed and experienced a devastating headache. She recalled writhing in pain, going through seizures, and hallucinating. She also suffered from blurred vision.

Schween received poor medical treatment in Russia; released from the hospital, she continued to exhibit symptoms at home, mostly memory loss and personality changes. She had other physical symptoms as well, including urinary tract infections and a wildly fluctuating heart rate and blood pressure.

Schween slowly recovered. To help their daughter return to normal, her parents committed themselves to her rehabilitation, exercising her brain by making her study hard, play math games, and memorize poetry. They also enlisted tutors to drill her in mathematics and other subjects. Eventually, she immigrated to Los Angeles, California, where she has attained college degrees in mathematics and biology and has become a research biologist. She has also established herself as an artist, specializing in photographic portraiture. Now twenty-five, Schween experiences occasional relapses, often manifested in emotional outbursts that doctors have attributed to her child-hood brain injury. "I don't think I will ever be a great scientist," she says, "but there is nothing I can't be successful at."[56]

Schween's success notwithstanding, her case shows that most brain trauma patients will suffer from some impairment of their cognitive functions for many years, if not for life. Lance Trexler, director of rehabilitation neuropsychology at the Rehabilitation Hospital of Indiana, states, "Not many people with moderate to severe injuries fully recover, in terms of the brain working exactly like it used to. About 50 percent do not resume their full activities and live with a chronic disability."[57]

Helmets, Seat Belts, and Air Bags

If Schween had been wearing a bicycle helmet at the time of her accident, the brain trauma she suffered as a child may have been much less severe, saving herself and her parents years of anguish and rehabilitation. According to the Arling-ton, Virginia–based Bicycle Helmet Safety Institute, of the 750 American bicyclists who die in accidents each year, some 75 percent succumb to head injuries. According to the institute, helmets can prevent 85 percent of the head injuries sustained by bicycle riders. Many skateboarders could avoid head inju-ries if they would also wear helmets. "You don't know how hard pavement is until your head really hits it," says an insti-tute publication. "If you [break] a wrist or an arm or a collar-bone it heals, but the brain is different."[58]

Safety experts urge athletes to wear helmets for all manner of other activities. Athletes who play contact sports such as football, ice hockey, lacrosse, and boxing are encouraged to wear helmets and, in fact, scholastic and community leagues often mandate head protection for participants. Many leagues require baseball and softball players to wear helmets when they bat and run the bases. Others who are urged by safety groups to wear helmets include in-line skaters, snowboarders, skiers, and horseback riders.

Many states do not require motorcycle riders to wear hel-mets, and, certainly, many riders resist the pleas of safety

Studies confirm that air bags can protect crash victims from serious head injuries.

experts to wear helmets as they race along on their cycles at speeds of 60 miles (96km) an hour or more. Safety experts encourage vehicle drivers and their passengers to wear seat belts and never drive under the influence of alcohol or drugs or ride with a driver under the influence.

Several studies have confirmed that people who wear seat belts and ride in vehicles equipped with front air bags suffer fewer head injuries than people who ride unrestrained. (Air bags were first installed in cars during the 1980s; they are typically hidden in the steering wheel and dashboard; during a collision they automatically inflate, providing a degree of protection to drivers and front-seat passengers.) In a head-on crash, an unrestrained body will be thrown forward—drivers and passengers may slam into the dashboard or windshield. A 2000 study by the Medical College of Wisconsin found that 10 percent of people who do not wear seat belts suffer head trauma when they are involved in front-end vehicular accidents. Meanwhile, the study found, in front-end accidents in which drivers and passengers are restrained by seat belts or protected by air bags, the TBI rate drops to less than 4 percent. The authors of another study claim:

> Air bags prevent the violent whiplash motion of the head in a frontal crash, resulting in a more controlled deceleration of the brain. Wrenching forces exerted on the cervical spine are [reduced], and the face is protected from contact with hard or lacerating surfaces. Furthermore, compliance is not a problem with air bags. When a car is equipped with air bags, they are in effect 100 percent of the time, which is important for the protection of high risk groups, such a teenage boys, who tend to wear seat belts less often than other groups.[59]

Unavoidable Mishaps

While many accidents that cause TBI occur on the roads, many mishaps also happen at home. People who live with elderly relatives are encouraged by safety experts to look around the house to see what may cause a slip—loose rugs or mats in the bathroom, for example. Poor lighting in the home can also cause mishaps. Safety experts urge parents of young children to install gates at the top of stairs and other unsafe places to help prevent falls. According to the National Center for Injury Prevention and Control, a division of the CDC, young children should continue to ride in juvenile car seats until they weigh about 40 pounds (18kg). The seats fit snugly around small children, providing them with extra protection should they get jostled in an accident. Also, the agency says, parents should inspect playgrounds to ensure that their surfaces are made of shock-absorbing materials, such as mulch or sand.

Of course, even the most vigilant attention to safety can't prevent all accidents. According to the Bicycle Helmet Safety Institute, even careful bike riders are likely to be involved in a crash every 4,500 miles (7,242km) of riding. Even though many riders wear helmets, traumatic brain injuries are still possible

Cyclists who do not wear helmets run the risk of a head injury if they crash.

if the impact is severe enough to shatter the plastic helmets or jar their brains inside their skulls. If they are well enough to pick themselves up off the street, they may still experience memory lapses, personality change, and long periods of rehabilitation ahead as they struggle to regain their former lives.

CHAPTER FIVE

The Future of Brain Trauma

The number of veterans of the Iraq and Afghanistan wars who have suffered traumatic brain injuries may be staggering, but the casualty count could have been a lot higher. Starting in late 2003 the military employed a newly designed helmet that has done a better job of deflecting and absorbing shrapnel than its predecessors. Known as the Advanced Combat Helmet, the headgear is composed of layers of Kevlar, a synthetic product that is stronger than steel but still retains an elastic quality. Therefore, the Kevlar layers can absorb more of the blow from a bomb blast without tearing. The helmet has even stopped direct shots from small arms, a feat unprecedented in helmet technology.

Adrian Danczyk's life was saved by an Advanced Combat Helmet. While serving in Iraq, Danczyk sustained a gunshot wound to the head. "I knew what had happened as soon as I was hit,"[60] Danczyk said. When examined by a medic, Danczyk was found to have suffered a minor cut only; his helmet had absorbed most of the impact from the gunshot.

The development of the Advanced Combat Helmet illustrates how technology is improving the odds for military personnel who are at risk of sustaining TBI. Elsewhere, engineers are working on new designs for football helmets and other headgear worn by athletes. The new designs are based on medical research that has provided a better understanding of how concussions and other brain injuries are caused. Meanwhile new instruments and surgical techniques are being employed in operating rooms, providing surgeons with tools that can make surgery less intrusive, giving many TBI patients better chances at recovery than they ever had before.

But better helmets and other protective devices only work if people use them. Across the country, the movement to make helmets mandatory for all motorcycle and bicycle riders has stalled. And though many soccer leagues are now requiring players to wear head protection, some soccer enthusiasts are skeptical about the effectiveness of headgear for players.

A soldier wears an Advanced Combat Helmet. The helmet, which does a better job of deflecting and absorbing shrapnel than its predecessors, is made of Kevlar and was introduced in late 2003.

Motorcyclist Deaths Increasing

A study by the National Highway Traffic Safety Administration concluded that while overall highway deaths have been declining in recent years, the number of fatalities involving motorcyclists has been spiraling upward. In 1997, the association reported, 2,116 motorcycle riders died in traffic accidents. In 2005 the number of fatalities involving motorcycle riders was recorded at 4,553—a 215 percent increase.

The administration said the death rate was 30 percent higher in states that do not require riders to wear helmets. In the 24 states that do not require helmets, 2,590 deaths were recorded in 2005 while in the 26 states and Washington, D.C., that do require helmets, 1,963 motorcyclists suffered fatal injuries. Says a statement by the Insurance Institute for Highway Safety, which lobbies for mandatory helmet laws:

> Motorcycles are less stable and less visible than cars and often have high performance capabilities. When motorcycles crash, their riders lack the protection of an enclosed vehicle, so they're more likely to be injured or killed. The federal government estimates that per mile traveled in 2005, the number of deaths on motorcycles was about 37 times the number in cars. . . .

During the past decade several states have repealed or weakened their helmet laws. In 1997 helmet laws in Texas and Arkansas were weakened to apply only to younger riders. Kentucky weakened its law in 1998, Florida weakened its law in 2000, and Pennsylvania weakened its law in 2003. Louisiana weakened its law in 1999 but reverted to universal coverage in 2004. Repealing or weakening helmet laws so they don't apply to all riders has been followed by increases in deaths. In contrast, benefits return when helmet laws applying to all riders are reinstated.

"Fatality Facts 2006: Motorcycles," Insurance Institute for Highway Safety. www.iihs.org/research/fatality_facts_2006/motorcycles.html.

Indeed, safety advocates know they still have a lot of work to do to persuade people to take simple precautions against what can be devastating injuries.

Blowing the Whistle on Concussions

In light of the brain trauma suffered by such high-profile stars as Andre Waters, Mike Webster, and Justin Strzelczyk, the National Football League has instituted some reforms designed to reduce the number of concussions suffered by players. In 2007 the NFL conducted a summit on concussions for team trainers, physicians, and other officials, providing them with the latest information on the causes and treatments of head injuries. Participants also exchanged ideas on how to better recognize head trauma in players who have always been reluctant to tell their trainers and coaches about on-field injuries.

Among the changes in league policy adopted as the result of the meeting was the establishment of regular neurological tests for all NFL players to determine whether they may be suffering from brain trauma. The tests are administered to the players prior to the season so that physicians can develop a baseline record of players' reactions and responses. By putting the athletes through a series of tests, physicians develop data on the attention span of the players as well as their motor coordination and balance. After the initial tests, the players are assessed again from time to time during the season to determine whether their abilities have deteriorated, which could indicate that they are showing the first subtle signs of brain injury. In the event a player sustains a concussion, doctors recommend holding him out of competition until the athlete's neurological signs reach preseason levels. That way players and team officials alike can be more confident that a player has completely healed before he resumes play. Many colleges have also adopted preseason neurological testing for players.

Another policy change that was adopted as a result of the concussion summit was a very simple change in league rules: All players are now required to snap their chin straps. It was a minor change in league rules, to be sure, but a helmet doesn't provide much protection unless it fits snugly on the head. Finally, the NFL established a "whistle-blower" program enabling any member of an NFL team to anonymously report players who take the field even though they may be suffering from brain trauma. Whistle-blowers are also encouraged to tell league officials about coaches they believe are pressuring brain-injured players to participate in games or practices. Troy Vincent, the president of the NFL Players Association, the union that represents professional football players, said the whistle-blower program may be helpful because players often have to be protected from themselves. "To ask a player with a head injury if he wants to go back into a game, that's not exactly the best thing," said Vincent. "Most players are going to make the emotional decision. They're going back onto the field."[61]

Advances in Helmet Design

Away from the field, equipment manufacturers are studying ways in which the design and manufacture of football helmets can be improved to minimize concussions. Indeed, football helmets have evolved a great deal since the first helmet was worn by a player in the 1893 Army-Navy game. That helmet was fashioned from leather by a shoemaker for a player who had already sustained head injuries and had been warned by a doctor that another severe blow to his head could cause permanent injury. Today regulation helmets are made of rigid plastic. In 2002 manufacturers altered the design of the helmets after a study found that most on-the-field concussions are caused by blows to the side of the head, rather than as a result of head-on collisions. The new design extended the helmet's protection to the jaw area and also increased padding, providing more distance between the head and the helmet so that more of the shock is absorbed by the padding. Manufacturers have made the new helmets available to professional, college, and high school teams.

Advances in helmet design are continuing. Some colleges have started using helmets equipped with sideline response

Football helmets have come a long way in design since they were first made of leather around the turn of the twentieth century.

system technology—electronic sensors that send signals to an off-the-field monitor that gauges the impact of a hit on a player's head. If the system detects a hit hard enough to cause a concussion, the team's medical staff is instructed to pull the player out of the game for an immediate evaluation. In fact, trainers and doctors standing on the sidelines are wired right into the system; when the buzzers hooked to their belts go off they know immediately that a player has been hit in the head too hard. Laptop computers wired into the system record the force of the hits and the identities of the players who sustain them. Since many players refuse to tell the medical staff about hard hits because they don't want to be pulled out of the game, the new technology will make it impossible for players to cover up their injuries. Other colleges plan to adopt the new helmets, and the NFL is also expected to introduce the helmets on a trial basis.

The University of Minnesota adopted the technology for its team in 2007. Defensive back Jamal Harris said he welcomes the device. Harris is known as a hard hitter. He has never suffered a concussion—at least he is not aware of ever suffering a concussion. Still, Harris said he is aware of the danger of head injury on the field. "It makes you feel better, so if I get my bell rung I know they're watching out for me," says Harris. "It makes me feel comfortable and everyone else feel comfortable. You know they don't want you to get hurt."[62]

At this point, only a handful of high schools have adopted the technology, mostly due to the high cost of the devices. It costs $1,000 to outfit each player's helmet as well as another $30,000 in equipment to monitor the impacts on the sidelines. One public school that has shouldered the expense is Tolono Unity High School near Champaign, Illinois. In 2007 the pagers and laptops alerted Tolono trainers to hard hits an average of three times a game, and helped the medical staff diagnose three concussions over the course of the team's first six games. One of those concussions was sustained by offensive tackle Jonathan Conlon. Struck hard in the head, Conlon wobbled back to the sidelines. By the time he made it to the bench, the medical staff had already concluded he suffered a concussion—the laptop computer told them so. "I guess I was kind of glad we had it," Conlon said of the device in his helmet. "If I didn't know how hard the hit was, I probably would have wanted to go back in the fourth quarter and maybe get hurt more."[63]

Soccer Headgear

There is no question that football is a contact sport that requires players to protect their heads. Many fans of soccer, on the other hand, don't regard the game as the type of sport that requires padding, including protective headgear. In light of the evidence that has surfaced linking TBI with heading the ball, however, many soccer leagues have started mandating that players must wear headgear as well. In 2003 the International Federation of Association Football, the world governing body for soccer, approved the use of headgear for soccer players;

that year, players in the Women's World Cup wore headgear for the first time, and in 2004 soccer players wore headgear for the first time in the Olympics.

In the United States many scholastic soccer teams as well as youth soccer associations have adopted the use of headgear, but not all soccer experts are sold on the equipment. The headgear resembles an enlarged headband. It is padded with shock-absorbing foam around the sides and back. In the United States soccer has often been promoted as a safe alternative to football. Some soccer enthusiasts fear that if headgear becomes mandatory for young players, parents will withdraw their children from the teams rather than risk any head injuries at all. Jeff Skeen, head of Full90, which manufactures headgear for soccer players, says, "They are trying to thwart the evolution of headgear in soccer because they think it will scare soccer moms away from the sign-up table and because they think it could be viewed as an admission that heading the ball itself is dangerous."[64]

Optional Gear

Off the athletic field, people who ride bicycles and motorcycles are now subject to a variety of laws regulating who must wear helmets. While many states have not enacted laws requiring motorcycle riders to wear helmets, city and local ordinances do make helmets mandatory. Some states allow adult riders to go helmetless but require young passengers to wear helmets. To date twenty-four states have no laws requiring motorcycle riders or passengers to wear helmets. Similarly, twenty-nine states do not require helmets for bicycle riders.

There is no nationally coordinated campaign to press for more comprehensive helmet laws or the establishment of helmet laws in states where none exist. Some groups representing motorcycle riders have successfully lobbied state lawmakers to sponsor legislation making helmets optional and, in some cases, the legislation has been adopted.

In 2003, for example, Pennsylvania lawmakers repealed the state's mandatory helmet law for motorcyclists. Five years

A road sign in Thailand warns motorcyclists that there is a fine for not wearing a helmet.

later the University of Pittsburgh released a study reporting that since repeal of the helmet law, the number of head-injury deaths in the state rose 32 percent. Despite this startling increase, state officials insist that motorcyclists should decide for themselves whether to wear helmets. Pennsylvania governor Edward Rendell's spokesman Chuck Ardo remarked, "The governor understands the statistics and he encourages all motorcycle riders to wear a helmet. But he believes it is a matter of personal choice."[65]

On the other hand, some states have enacted stricter helmet laws, often at the urging of insurers. In 1999, for example, Louisiana repealed its mandatory helmet law, then reinstated it five years later after the death rate for motorcyclists increased by 100 percent. Advocates of stricter helmet laws have settled in for a long, state-by-state campaign that, at least for now, appears to be making little progress.

The campaign to adopt mandatory helmet laws in America may be stumbling along, but that is not the case in other countries—particularly places where motorcycle and motor-bike riding is a main form of transportation. In Vietnam, for example, motorcycles and motorbikes account for some 90 percent of all traffic on the country's roads. By 2007 the death toll from motorcycle and motorbike accidents stood at a stag-gering thirty a day. Rose Moxham, an Australian living in the Vietnamese capital of Hanoi, witnessed a fatal accident: A group of motorcycle riders were stopped at a red light when they were struck from behind by a rider who failed to stop. One woman sitting atop her motorbike waiting for the light to change was knocked over. Her head struck the ground. "She dropped her bike, fell off, hit her head on the road and died," said Moxham. "Just like that. Dead."[66]

In response to such incidents, the Vietnamese government has mandated that all motorcycle and motorbike riders must wear helmets. Prior to enactment of the law, it was estimated that fewer than 10 percent of riders in Vietnam wore helmets. Since establishment of the law, traumatic brain injuries caused by traffic accidents have been reduced by nearly 30 percent. Etienne Krug, director of Violence and Injury Prevention for the World Health Organization in Geneva, Switzerland, con-tends, "The countries that adopt and enforce helmet legislation reduce injuries and deaths. And the states that repeal them see an increase. It's just a fact."[67]

No Bans on Pro Boxing

Another organized effort that seems to have stalled is the movement to outlaw professional boxing. (Several features of amateur boxing significantly reduce the risk of TBI. Amateur bouts are limited to four rounds instead of the ten or twelve rounds in traditional professional bouts. All amateur partici-pants wear headgear and the goal of the competitors is not to knock out or bloody an opponent, but to score points by land-ing punches. Nevertheless, many amateur boxers eventually find themselves at risk of TBI because they turn professional.)

The American Medical Association (AMA) has been on record since 1983 calling for a professional boxing ban. Professional boxing is typically policed by state athletic commissions that establish their own rules for regulating bouts and ensuring the safety of the fighters. Each state has set its own rules regarding the weight and padding required in boxing gloves, important factors in the cause of head trauma. Moreover, in recent years a new version of boxing known as ultimate fighting or mixed martial arts has gained popularity. Perhaps even more brutal than boxing, ultimate fighting permits head-butting, kicking, and almost any other tactic a competitor might use to bloody and knock out an opponent. State athletic commissions are now policing those competitions as well. In 2003 U.S. senator John McCain, who fought as an amateur while attending the U.S. Naval Academy, proposed legislation giving the federal

The brutality of the sport of professional boxing has caused the American Medical Association to recommend that it be banned.

government authority over the sport of boxing. The act would establish a federal boxing commissioner as well as one set of rules for all professional boxing, but the legislation has failed to gain support in Washington. Marc Ratner, executive director of the Nevada State Athletic Commission, states, "The U.S. government has a lot more to worry about than the sport of boxing."[68]

In the meantime, no state has banned boxing but doctors still speak out. George A. Lundberg, the Louisville, Kentucky, physician who wrote the original AMA editorial calling for a ban on boxing, said that a knockout renders the opponent unconscious, which is a form of brain trauma. "That is morally just flat wrong,"[69] he says.

Advances in Medicine

As politicians wrestle with legislative issues, advances in medicine have improved the prognoses for many TBI patients. A new robotic arm guided by brain surgeons, for example, can perform microsurgery with far more precision than a surgeon can achieve with his or her hands. During the procedure the surgeon's fingers do not enter the brain of the patient. Rather, the surgeon controls the robotic device from a computer terminal in another room. To perform the surgery the physician works from a map of the brain provided by a real-time MRI scan. The MRI provides surgeons with more detail than they can see with their eyes. The robotic surgery has been performed in Calgary, Alberta, by neurosurgeon Garnette Sutherland, who has compared it to playing a video game. "We would all agree that our young children who have become immersed in video games represent the future generation of surgeons,"[70] Sutherland says.

Meanwhile, new imaging equipment developed in part by the National Aeronautics and Space Administration (NASA) provides neurosurgeons with three-dimensional images of the brain, actually enabling physicians to look into crevices and around corners in the brain before cutting. The device is similar to an endoscope, a tiny camera that has been used for decades to provide images of human anatomy. NASA has helped develop the technology because a version of the camera may be used on future Mars landing missions.

Neurologists are also developing techniques to better assess patients in persistent vegetative states, and in some cases their prognoses are more optimistic. In the past neurologists gauged a patient's reaction to noise as a method of determining whether the patient was hopelessly in a vegetative state. Now neurologists are finding some patients respond when they hear familiar sounds—such as the patient's name or a family member's voice. It means that the patients may have a slim chance of recovery instead of no hope at all. "We know from extensive research that brain responses of this type do not occur automatically," says British neurologist Adrian Owen, adding that a vegetative patient's response to a voice "require[s] the willed, intentional action of the participant."[71]

Robotic surgery now allows surgeons to perform operations from a computer terminal while the patient is in an MRI machine.

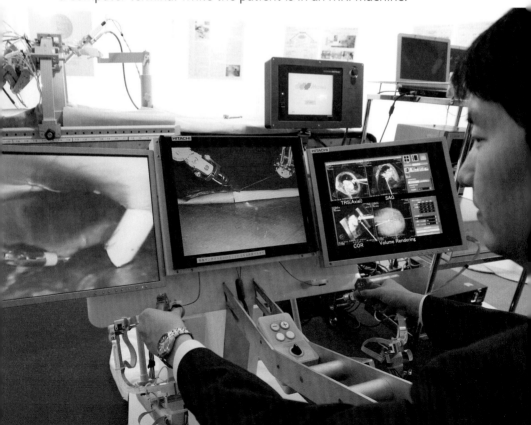

Stem Cells and Brain Trauma

Stem cell research holds a lot of promise for traumatic brain injury patients, according to research performed at the University of California (UC) at Irvine. According to the 2007 study, mice with brain injuries demonstrated improvements in memory within three months of receiving the stem cell treatments.

Stem cell therapy uses cells at the very earliest stage of development—from unimplanted embryos at in-vitro fertilization clinics, umbilical cords and placental tissue at birth, and cells withdrawn from aborted fetuses—because research has shown that these cells are undifferentiated "blank" cells that can develop into all kinds of different tissue and organs for many different therapeutic purposes. Stem cells have the potential to replace damaged or diseased cells. Many conservative politicians and the antiabortion movement oppose embryonic stem cell research, however, arguing that embryos are persons and the research destroys human life. The controversy continues; meanwhile, stem cell research has been slowed in America because the federal government has refused to provide grants to universities and institutions conducting research.

Still, research has continued without federal aid. At UC Irvine, neurobiologist Frank LaFerla said, "Our research provides clear evidence that stem cells can reverse memory loss. This gives us hope that stem cells someday could help restore brain function in humans suffering from a wide range of diseases and injuries that impair memory formation."

A light microscope shows human embryonic stem cells. Stem cell research has shown promise for traumatic brain injury patients.

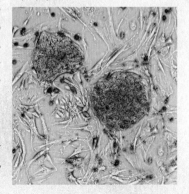

Quoted in "Stem Cells Can Improve Memory After Brain Injury," *Science Daily*, November 2, 2007. www.sciencedaily.com/releases/2007/10/071030184522.htm.

Medical technology that can help traumatic brain injury patients may be advancing, but there is no question that TBI remains a frightful, heart-wrenching, and devastating disability. Abundant evidence proves that motorcycle riders, bicyclists, and others can avoid traumatic brain injuries by wearing their helmets. Meanwhile, doctors and team trainers continue to counsel young athletes to recognize the warning signs of concussion and to realize that taking a seat on the bench may be the wisest way to respond to a blow to the head.

Notes

Introduction: Brain Trauma: The Invisible Epidemic

1. Quoted in Neil Shea, "The Heroes, the Healing: Military Medicine, from the Front Lines to the Home Front," *National Geographic*, December 2006. http://ngm.national geographic.com/ngm/0612/feature3/index.html.
2. Quoted in Shea, "The Heroes, the Healing."
3. Quoted in Alan Schwarz, "Expert Ties Ex-Player's Suicide to Brain Damage from Football," *New York Times*, January 18, 2007, p. A1.
4. Quoted in Schawrz, "Expert Ties Ex-Player's Suicide to Brain Damage from Football," p. A1.
5. Quoted in Christopher Nowinski, "Headed for Trouble?" *Sports Illustrated*, October 13, 2006. http://sportsillus trated.cnn.com/2006/writers/the_bonus/10/12/morgan. concussions/index.html.
6. Quoted in Nowinski, "Headed for Trouble?"

Chapter One: What Is Brain Trauma?

7. Michael Paul Mason, *Head Cases: Stories of Brain Injury and Its Aftermath*. New York: Farrar, Straus and Giroux, 2008, pp. 6–7.
8. Quoted in Eric Fengler, "The Science of Head Injury," *Bicycling*, October 2007, p. 64.
9. Quoted in Kirsten Weir, "Hard Knocks," *Current Science*, September 21, 2007, p. 8.
10. Quoted in Wallace Matthews, "Boxing's Johnson, 35, Dies. Injuries Prove Fatal Five Days After His Lightweight Bout vs. Chaves Was Stopped," *Newsday*, September 23, 2005, p. A87.
11. Quoted in Ira Berkow, "Two Years After Brain Injury, Mesi Earns Victory and Relief," *New York Times*, April 2, 2006, pp. 8–10.

12. Mason, *Head Cases*, p. 71.
13. Quoted in "What Is Neurosurgery?" *Neurosurgery Today*, American Association of Neurological Surgeons, June 2006. www.neurosurgerytoday.org/what/patient_e/head.asp.

Chapter Two: How Do Brains Get Traumatized?

14. Quoted in Polly Shuman, "Blowing the Whistle on Concussions," *Scientific American Presents*, 2000, p. 44.
15. Quoted in Shuman, "Blowing the Whistle on Concussions," p. 44.
16. Quoted in Stan Grossfeld, "Bergeron Recovering from a Concussion, but Hits Keep on Coming," *Boston Globe*, April 4, 2008, p. E1.
17. Quoted in Grossfeld, "Bergeron Recovering from a Concussion, but Hits Keep on Coming," p. E-1.
18. Quoted in Bob DiCesare, "Dangerous Games: Athletes, Especially Young People, Are at Great Risk for Concussion," *Buffalo News*, August 5, 2001, p. A1.
19. Quoted in DiCesare, "Dangerous Games," p. A1.
20. Quoted in "Boy Suffers Brain Injury, Dies After Heading a Ball," *Harrisburg Patriot*, September 5, 1996, p. A1.
21. Quoted in "Head Impact and Sports," *Pediatrics for Parents*, 2000, p. 1.
22. Quoted in DiCesare, "Dangerous Games," p. A1.
23. Quoted in Robert L. Smith, "School Superintendent to Return to Job Part Time," *Syracuse Post-Standard*, January 11, 1996, p. 3.
24. Quoted in Beth Vrabel, "Teen's Recovery from Brain Injury a Miracle: A Central York High School Grad Was in a Coma for a Week After an ATV Accident," *York (PA) Daily Record*, August 9, 2005, p. 5.
25. Quoted in Mason, *Head Cases*, p. 211.
26. Quoted in Ian Herbert, "Richards Concussed After Fall from Coconut Tree," *London Independent*, May 1, 2006. www.independent.co.uk/arts-entertainment/music/news/richards-concussed-after-fall-from-coconut-tree-476340.html.

27. Quoted in Gregg Zoroya, "Key Iraq Wound: Brain Trauma," *USA Today*, March 3, 2005. www.usatoday.com/news/nation/2005-03-03-brain-trauma-lede_x.htm.
28. Quoted in Thomas Fields-Meyer et al., "After Iraq, Devastating New Wounds," *People*, May 9, 2005, p. 223.
29. Quoted in Gregg Zoroya, "Brain Injuries Range from Loss of Coordination to Loss of Self," *USA Today*, March 3, 2005. www.usatoday.com/news/nation/2005-03-03-brain-injuries-inside_x.htm?loc=interstatialskip.
30. Shea, "The Heroes, the Healing."

Chapter Three: Living with Brain Trauma

31. U.S. Centers for Disease Control and Prevention, *Traumatic Brain Injury in the United States: A Report to Congress*, December 1999. www.cdc.gov/ncipc/tbi/tbi_congress/tbi_congress.htm.
32. Quoted in Greg Logan, "Concussions in Sports: Damaging Blows for Boxing," *Newsday*, July 10, 1996, p. A58.
33. Quoted in Richard Goldstein, "Jerry Quarry, 53, Boxer Battered by Years in the Ring, Dies," *New York Times*, January 5, 1999, p. A15.
34. Stanley M. Aronson, "Should Dr. Alzheimer Have Been a Boxing Fan?" *Providence Journal*, June 25, 2007, p. C5.
35. Quoted in Beth Harris, Associated Press, "Mike Quarry, March 4, 1951–June 11, 2006; Light Heavyweight Contender from Boxing Family," *Pittsburgh Post-Gazette*, June 14, 2006, p. E6.
36. Quoted in M.W. Van Allen, "Boxing Should Be Banned," *Saturday Evening Post*, May/June 1992, p. 60.
37. Quoted in Walter Sullivan, "Many Boxers Found Afflicted," *New York Times*, September 23, 1984, p. A11.
38. Quoted in Tim Dahlberg, Associated Press, "Now It's Up to Others to Talk for Him; Former Heavyweight Champion Looks His Age as He Turns 65," *Albany Times Union*, January 17, 2007, p. C1.
39. Quoted in Don Pierson, "It Was Game That Claimed Ex-Steeler," *Chicago Tribune*, September 25, 2002, p. 1.
40. Quoted in Nowinski, "Headed for Trouble?"

41. Quoted in Steve Maich, "The Concussion Time Bomb," *Maclean's*, October 22, 2007, p. 46.

42. Quoted in Gene Warner, "The School of Hard Knocks; Former Wrestler Tells Tale of Suffering Too Many Concussions," *Buffalo News*, February 13, 2007, p. B1.

43. Quoted in Fields-Meyer et al., "After Iraq, Devastating New Wounds," p. 223.

44. Steven Laureys, "Eyes Open, Brain Shut," *Scientific American*, May 2007, p. 86.

45. Quoted in Carey Goldberg, "After a Coma: Comebacks Are Slow and Patchy, and Almost Never Miraculous," *Boston Globe*, July 5, 2005, p. E1.

46. U.S. Centers for Disease Control and Prevention, *Traumatic Brain Injury in the United States: A Report to Congress.*

47. Quoted in Fields-Meyer et al., "After Iraq, Devastating New Wounds," p. 223.

Chapter Four: Treating and Preventing Brain Trauma

48. Quoted in Fengler, "The Science of Head Injury," p. 64.

49. Mason, *Head Cases*, pp. 242–43.

50. Mason, *Head Cases*, p. 169.

51. Quoted in Karen Kaplan, "Doctors Say Man Awoke After His Brain Rebuilt Itself," *Pittsburgh Post-Gazette*, July 4, 2006, p. A1.

52. Quoted in Jan Hoffman, "Coaching the Comeback," *New York Times*, January 15, 2008, p. F1.

53. Quoted in Hoffman, "Coaching the Comeback," p. F1.

54. Quoted in Shea, "The Heroes, the Healing."

55. Quoted in Shea, "The Heroes, the Healing."

56. Quoted in Mason, *Head Cases*, p. 108.

57. Quoted in Fengler, "The Science of Head Injury," p. 64.

58. Bicycle Helmet Safety Institute, "Skateboard Helmets," January 1, 2008. www.helmets.org/skatepam.htm.

59. J. Jagger, K. Vernberg, and J. Jane, "Air Bags: Reducing the Toll of Brain Trauma," *Neurosurgery*, May 1987, p. 815.

Chapter Five : The Future of Brain Trauma

60. Quoted in Terry Boyd, "New Helmet Design Credited with Saving Soldier's Life," *Stars and Stripes*, October 31,

2004. www.stripes/com/article.asp?section=104&article=2 4358&archive=true.

61. Quoted in Len Pasquarelli, "Concussion Policy to Include 'Whistle-Blower' Provision," ESPN, June 19, 2007. http://sports.espn.go.com/nfl/news/story?id=2909463.

62. Quoted in Chip Scoggins, "Tackling Concussions," *Minneapolis Star Tribune*, August 9, 2007.

63. Quoted in Barry Temkin, "Hard-Hitting Research on Concussions," *Chicago Tribune*, October 5, 2007, p. 16.

64. Quoted in Jere Longman, "Soccer Headgear: Does It Do Any Good?" *New York Times*, November 27, 2004, p. D1.

65. Quoted in Melissa Dribben, "Vietnam Shows Effect of Motorcycle Helmets," *Philadelphia Inquirer*, June 28, 2008, p. A1.

66. Quoted in Dribben, "Vietnam Shows Effect of Motorcycle Helmets," p. A1.

67. Quoted in Dribben, "Vietnam Shows Effect of Motorcycle Helmets," p. A1.

68. Quoted in Kathleen Murphy, "Federal Oversight Urged for State Boxing Commissions," Stateline.org, February 26, 2003. www.stateline.org/live/ViewPage.action?siteNodeId =136&languageId=1&contentId=15170.

69. Quoted in Jim Adams, "Push for Ban on Boxing Is Still Hotly Debated," *Louisville Courier-Journal*, May 4, 2007. www.courier-journal.com/apps/pbs.dll/article?AD=2007105040008.

70. Quoted in "Calgary Woman Recovering After Robotic Arm Removes Brain Tumor," CBC, May 16, 2008. www.cbc.ca/technology/story/2008/05/16/robotic-surgery.html.

71. Quoted in Sharon Begley, "There May Be More to a Vegetative State than Science Thought," *Wall Street Journal*, September 8, 2006, p. B1.

Glossary

clot: Mass of dried blood that can compress and damage sensitive brain tissue.

computed tomography scan: Also known as a CT scan (and sometimes as a computed axial tomography scan, or CAT scan) the device converts X-rays into electrical impulses to produce a three-dimensional image of the brain.

concussion: A mild form of traumatic brain injury; a concussion usually involves a shifting of the brain inside the skull.

depression: Mood disorder characterized by feelings of sadness, hopelessness, and inadequacy.

electroencephalogram: Known as an EEG, the test measures electrical activity in the brain.

hemorrhage: Heavy bleeding due to ruptured blood vessels.

infarction: Tissue death caused by a blockage of blood and oxygen to the tissue, occuring most commonly in the heart (myocardial infarction).

magnetic resonance imaging: Known as an MRI, this test uses a doughnut-shaped magnet to energize atoms in human cells that are detected by radio waves, producing an image of the organ or tissue being scanned.

neurologist: Physician specializing in treatment of diseases and injuries to the nerves, especially those of the central nervous system, which includes the brain and spinal cord.

neurosurgeon: Physician specializing in brain surgery.

pathologist: Physician specializing in determining the origin of disease; the pathologist usually conducts laboratory analyses of tissue and organs.

second-impact syndrome: Rare condition that can afflict athletes and others who suffer successive concussions, occurring because their brains have not yet recovered from the initial concussions when they receive additional jolts. This syndrome involves sudden, usually fatal brain swelling.

subdural hematoma: Bleeding inside the skull but not actually in the brain; hematomas can cause pressure inside the skull that can damage the brain.

Organizations to Contact

American Association of Neurological Surgeons

5550 Meadowbrook Dr.
Rolling Meadows, IL 60008
phone: (888) 566-2267
fax: (847) 378-0600
e-mail: info@aans.org
Web site: www.aans.org

Representing doctors who specialize in brain surgery, the association promotes neurosurgery as a science and publishes the *Journal of Neurosurgery*, which contains articles outlining the latest advances in brain surgery. Visitors to the organization's Web site can find statistics about neurosurgery, news reports about brain injuries, and press releases outlining the society's efforts to advance the science of neurosurgery.

Bicycle Helmet Safety Institute

4611 Seventh St. South
Arlington, VA 22204-1419
phone: (703) 486-0100
e-mail: info@helmets.org
Web site: www.bhsi.org

The institute serves as an advocate for the use of bicycle helmets by all riders. Visitors to the organization's Web site can find extensive information on how to select a helmet, which states require riders to wear helmets, and statistics on head injuries sustained by riders who do not wear helmets.

Brain Injury Association of America

1608 Spring Hill Rd., Ste. 110
Vienna, VA 22182

phone: (703) 761-0750
fax: (703) 761-0755
e-mail: info@biausa.org
Web site: www.biausa.org

The association serves as an advocacy group for brain injury patients and their families. The group has helped win government grants for research and rehabilitation projects and has published guides for families and others whose lives are touched by traumatic brain injuries. Visitors to the association's Web site can read stories of how brain injury patients endured their rehabilitations.

Brain Trauma Foundation
708 Third Ave.
New York, NY 10017
phone: (212) 772-0608
Web site: www.braintrauma.org

The foundation was established to support medical research and provide education to physicians about traumatic brain injury. Visitors to the foundation's Web site can find statistics about traumatic brain injury (TBI) in the United States as well as an archive of news articles about the latest developments in brain trauma research.

Centers for Disease Control and Prevention
Office of Communication
1600 Clifton Rd. NE, Bldg. 16, D-42
Atlanta, GA 30333
phone: (800) 311-3435
e-mail: cdcinfo@cdc.gov
Web site: www.cdc.gov

The federal government's chief public health agency explores trends in diseases and other conditions that affect the health of Americans. The National Center for Injury Prevention and Control, an agency of the CDC, maintains an extensive archive of information on traumatic brain injury on its Web site.

National Institute of Mental Health

6001 Executive Blvd.
Bethesda, MD 20892-9663
phone: (866) 615-6464
e-mail: nimhinfo@nih.gov
Web site: www.nimh.nih.gov

The National Institute of Mental Health is the federal government's chief funding agency for mental health research in America. Students can find many resources about mental illnesses caused by traumatic brain injury, including depression and attention disorder, by visiting the agency's Web site.

National Institute of Neurological Disorders and Stroke

PO Box 5801
Bethesda, MD 20824
phone: (800) 352-9424
Web site: www.ninds.nih.gov

An agency of the National Institutes of Health, the organization promotes research into traumatic brain injury. Visitors to the agency's Web site can find a description of traumatic brain injury, explanation of methods of treatment and rehabilitation, and the status of research into the causes of TBI.

For Further Reading

Books

Robert S. Gotlin, ed., *Sports Injuries Guidebook: Athletes' and Coaches' Resource for Identification, Treatment and Recovery*. Champaign, IL: Human Kinetics, 2008. The editor, a physician, has included an extensive chapter on concussions and other head injuries, providing athletes and their coaches with information on the symptoms they may encounter after sustaining head trauma on the field.

Michael Paul Mason, *Head Cases: Stories of Brain Injury and Its Aftermath*. New York: Farrar, Straus, and Giroux, 2008. A social worker who helps brain trauma patients put their lives back together discusses interesting cases while giving readers a thorough overview of brain trauma and its treatments.

Louisa Ray Morningstar, *Journey Through Brain Trauma: A Mother's Story of Her Daughter's Recovery*. Lanham, MD: Taylor Trade, 1998. The author's daughter, Misti Morningstar, sustained severe brain trauma in an automobile accident. The author tells the story in the form of a diary, as she recounts Misti's long and difficult recovery from brain trauma.

Chris Nowinski, *Head Games: Football's Concussion Crisis from the NFL to Youth Leagues*. Plymouth, MA: Drummond, 2006. The author, a former college football player and professional wrestler, sustained numerous concussions, forcing him to give up his athletic career. Nowinski talks about his own symptoms of brain trauma and explores how professional football players and other athletes have ignored the dangers of brain trauma by returning to the field too soon after suffering concussions.

Periodicals

Eric Fengler, "The Science of Head Injury," *Bicycling*, October 2007. The author provides a thorough overview of head injuries typically sustained by bicycle enthusiasts.

Thomas Fields-Meyer et al., "After Iraq, Devastating New Wounds," *People*, May 9, 2005. A report on the large number of head wounds suffered by soldiers and marines serving in Iraq.

Karen Kaplan, "Doctors Say Man Awoke After His Brain Rebuilt Itself," *Pittsburgh Post Gazette*, July 4, 2006. The story of Terry Wallis, the Arkansas man who emerged from a minimally conscious state eighteen years after suffering traumatic brain injury in a vehicular accident.

Jere Longman, "Soccer Headgear: Does It Do Any Good?" *New York Times*, November 27, 2004. Examines the debate over the effectiveness of headgear for soccer players, who could sustain traumatic brain injuries while heading the ball.

Steve Maitz, "The Concussion Time Bomb," *Maclean's*, October 22, 2007. The Canadian weekly newsmagazine reports on the cases of former NFL star Justin Strzelczyk and pro wrestler Chris Benoit, both of whom died violently. Experts conclude both men suffered from severe brain trauma following numerous concussions.

Alan Schwarz, "Expert Ties Ex-player's Suicide to Brain Damage from Football," *New York Times*, January 18, 2007. The findings of pathologist Bennet Omalu, who concluded that former NFL star Andre Waters's depression and suicide were caused by numerous concussions sustained during his football career.

Web Sites

The American Crowbar Case (www.neurosurgery.org/cy bermuseum/pre20th/crowbar/crowbar.html). Maintained by the American Association of Neurological Surgeons, the site includes a history of the Phineas Gage case; Gage was a nineteenth-century railroad worker who survived a traumatic brain injury in which a steel bar pierced his skull.

History of Brain Surgery (www.brain-surgery.com/history.html). Maintained by neurosurgeons at New York University Medical Center, the site provides students with an overview of the history of brain surgery, starting with efforts by Egyptian physicians more than thirty-five hundred years ago.

Motorcycle and Bicycle Helmet Laws (www.iihs.org/laws/ HelmetUseCurrent.aspx). Maintained by the Insurance Institute for Highway Safety, the site provides a state-by-state guide to laws requiring the use of helmets by motorcycle and bicycle riders.

Sports Legacy Institute (www.sportslegacy.org). Web site for the organization established by former college football player and pro wrestler Chris Nowinski, an advocate for athletes who suffer from traumatic brain injury. The institute maintains an archive of news articles about concussions, updates on recent brain injury research, and information on how the families of deceased athletes can donate their brain tissue to medical research.

Index

A
Accidents, 34
  falls, *33*, 33–34, 36, 67–68
  motor vehicle, 34–36, *36*, 55,
    61–63, 68–70
  preventing, 70
  protective headgear and, 32,
    70–71, *71*, 73
Advanced Combat Helmet, 72, *73*
Afghanistan, 28, 37–39, 72
Air bags (car), *69*, 69–70
Ali, Lonnie, 46
Ali, Muhammad, 41, 44–46, *45*
Alzheimer's disease, 7–8, 40–41,
  45–46
*American Journal of Sports
  Medicine*, 32
American Medical Association
  (AMA), 81–83
Anderson, Robert, 33–34
Angiograms, 22–23
Ardo, Chuck, 80
Aronson, Stanley M., 43
Atlas, Teddy, 19
Axons, 12, *13*

B
Battlefield medicine, 37
Baun, Willie, 15–16
Benoit, Chris, *47*, 48
Bicyclists
  helmets and, 27, 68, 70–71, *71*,
    73, 79
  percent of traumatic brain injuries
    (TBIs), 34
Body armor, 37
Boxing, 17–19, 41–46, *42*, *45*, 81–83,
  82
Brain, 12–14, 16–19, *17*, 56–57, 61–63
  See also Neurons
Brain dead, 52

C
Calcium, 15
Car seats, 70
Children
  contact sports and, 30–32, *31*
  falls and, 67–68
  protecting, 70
  shaken baby syndrome (SBS), 27
Closed head trauma, 11, 12
  See also Concussions
Comas
  assessing degree of trauma, 18
  described, 51
  long-term problems, 10–11
  recovery potential, 55
  SBS and, 27
Computed (axial) tomography (CT/
  CAT) scans, 21–22, 23, 30, 61
Concussions, 16
  effects, 10
    calcium buildup, 15
    immediate, 29, 30
    short-term, 9, 16
  grading scale, 14
  multiple, 7–8, 15, 25–26
  NFL reforms to reduce, 75–76
  recovery from, 32
  sideline response system
    technology and, 76–78
  See also Disabilities
Conlon, Jonathan, 78
Consciousness
  loss of, 14
  minimal, 53, 55
Contact sports. *See specific sports*
Cosell, Howard, 44–45
Costs, annual, 55
Cramner, Ron, 42

D
Danczyk, Adrian, 72

Deaths
  annual, 36
  of bicyclists, 68
  decline in rate, 61
  from hematomas, 18
  of motorcyclists, 74, 81
  from second-impact syndrome
    (SIS), 15
  from youth soccer, 30
Dementia, 40, 42
Dementia pugilistica, 43, 44, 47–48,
  49
Dendrites, 12
Depression, 7–8, 41, 47–48
Diagnosis
  of closed head TBI, *20*, 20–23
  equipment advances, 83–84
  of open head TBI, 19
DiBella, Lou, 19
DiBlasi, Rick, Jr., 29
DiBlasi, Rick, Sr., 29
Disabilities
  annual increase in number with, 40
  chronic, 67–68
  cognitive, 65–66
  dementia, 40, 42
  dementia pugilistica, 43, 44, 47, 49
  physical, 35–36, 37, 62–63, 64–65
  psychological, 7–8, 37, 41, 47–48,
    49–51
  from SBS, 27
  See also Comas

E
Electroencephalograms (EEGs),
  22, 52
Embryonic stem cells, 85, *85*
End-of-life decisions, 51–53, 54
Eye examinations, 20, *20*

F
Falls, *33*, 33–34, 36, 67–68, 70
Families of victims
  effects on, 40–41, 55
  end-of-life decisions and, 51–53,
    54
Felteau, Melissa, 35–36
First responders, 57–58
Football players
  concussions and, 7, 8, 15–16

dementia pugilistica, 47–48
helmet design, 76–78, *77*
personality changes, 49–50, *50*
pre-season neurological tests,
  75

G
Gage, Phineas, 66
Gamma Knife radiosurgery, 60–61
Glasgow Coma Scale (GCS), 18
Gless, Alec, 50–51, 55
Gless, Shana, 51, 55
The Greatest, 41, 44–46, *45*

H
Harlow, John, 66
Harris, Jamal, 78
Helmets/headgear
  accidents when wearing, 70–71,
    71
  design, 72–73, 76–78, *77*
  importance of, 27, 29, 68, 74
  laws, 68, 73, 74, 79–81, *80*
  soccer and, 78–79
  use of, 31, 32, 69, 73, 75–76
  war wounds and, 72, *73*
Hemorrhages, 13–14, 16
Hockey players, 25–26, *26*, 28, *29*,
  29–30
Hoge, Merril, 8–9
Holmes, Larry, 44–45
Hospitalization, 61

I
Improvised explosive devices
  (IEDs), 28
Individual rights, 54
Infants, 27
Insomnia, 41
Intracranial pressure (ICP)
  monitoring, 23–24

J
Johnson, Leavander, 17–19
*Journal of the American Medical
  Association*, 43
*Journal of Trauma, Injury,
  Infection, and Critical Care*, 31

K
Kaelin, Darryl, 56–57

Kessler Institute for Rehabilitation, 64–65
Kevlar, 72, *73*
Klein, Andrew, 34–35
Krug, Etienne, 81

L
Ladders, *33*, 33–34
LaFerla, Frank, 85
Laureys, Steven, 51
Levin, Jodi, 64–65
Lindros, Brett, 28
Lindros, Eric, 25–26, *26*, 28
Living wills, 52–53, 54
Louisiana, 80
Lundberg, George A., 83
Lux, Warren, 65

M
Magnetic resonance imaging (MRI), 22, *23*, 61, 83
Martial arts, 82
Martland, Harrison S., 43
Mason, Michael Paul, 10–11, 19
    on brain self-recovery, 61
    on brain surgery in Iraq, 59
McCain, John, 82–83
Melton, Mark, 59
Memory loss, 10, 12–13
    from accidents, 35, 67
    from football, 47
    rehabilitation therapy for, 65–66
    stem cells and, 85
    from stroke, 16
    from war wounds, 37, 50, 67
Meninges, 12, 19
Mesi, Joe, 19
Microsurgery, 83, *84*
Migraine headaches, 41
Mitchell, David, 38–39
Montmarquet, Jessica, 30
Montmarquet, Kathy, 30
Motor vehicle accidents, 34–36, *36*, 55, 61–63, 68–70, 73
Motorcyclists
    deaths, 74, 81
    helmet laws and, 68–69, 73, 74, 79–81, *80*
    percent of TBIs, 34

Moxham, Rose, 81

N
National Aeronautics and Space Administration (NASA), 83–84
National Football League (NFL) reforms, 75–76
Neurons
    Alzheimer's disease and, 45–46
    blood supply to, 16, 57
    calcium buildup in, 15
    death of, 14
    function, 12
    parkinsonism/Parkinson's disease and, 46
Neurosurgery, 58
Nowinski, Chris, 8, 49

O
Occupational therapy, *64*, 64–65
Omalu, Bennet, 48
Open head trauma, 11, 19
Ophthalmoscopes, 20, *20*
Owen, Adrian, 84

P
Paramedics, 57–58
Parkinsonism, 45–46
Parkinson's disease, 45–46
Pearson, Robert, 44
Pennsylvania, 79–80
Persistent vegetative states (PVSs), 51–53, *53*, 55, 84
Personality changes, 37
    historic example, 66
    mental illness, 7–8, 41, 47–48, 49–51
    rehabilitation for, 65–67
    violence, 48
Playgrounds, 70
Punch drunk, 43

Q
Quarry, Jerry, 41–43, *42*, 44, 45
Quarry, Mike, 44
Quinlan, Joseph, 54, *54*
Quinlan, Julia, 54, *54*
Quinlan, Karen Ann, 54

R
Ratner, Marc, 83
Rehabilitation therapy, 56–57, 63–68
Repetitive head injury, 15
Richards, Keith, 36
Right to die, 54
Robotic microsurgery, 83, *84*
Rogers, Linda, 43
Rutland, Justin, 30
Rutland-Simpson, Jiea, 30

S
Sass, Brian, 55
Sass, Lorelei, 55
Schiavo, Terri, 53, *53*
Schiff, Nicholas, 63
Schween, Asya, 67–68
Seat belts, 69–70
Second-impact syndrome (SIS),
    15
Shaken Baby Syndrome (SBS), 27
Shea, Neil, 38–39
Sideline response system
    technology, 76–78
Silver, Tim, 37
Sims, John, 37
Sims, Violeta, 37
Skateboarders, 68
Skeen, Jeff, 79
Skull, 12, 17
Slap happy, 43
Slug nutty, 43
Smith, Edwin, 58
Smith, Ross, 37
Smith Papyrus, 58
Soccer
    amateur, 30–32, *31*
    headgear, 78–79
    mandatory helmet use, 73
Social skills, 50–51
    See also Dementia
Speech therapy, 63
Sports. *See specific sports*
Stem cell therapy, 85, *85*
Stigma, 7
Strokes, 16, 17, 23
Strzelczyk, Justin, 49–50, *50*
Subdural hematomas, *17*, 17–19
Surgery, 56, *57*, 58–61, *60*, 83, *84*

Sutherland, Garnette, 83

T
Teenagers
    football and, 15–16, 78
    hockey and, 29–30
    motor vehicle accidents and,
        34–35
    risk for TBIs, 6, 35
    soccer and, 30–32, *31*, 79
Thailand, *80*
Traumatic brain injury (TBI), *11*
    annual number sustained, 6, 16
    categories, 11, 12, 19
    defined, 10
    most common causes, 34
    overview of, 6–7
    types, 10
Trexler, Lance, 12, 68

U
Ultimate fighting, 82
Ultrasound equipment, 59–60

V
Vietnam, 81
Vincent, Troy, 76

W
Wallis, Terry, 61–63, *62*
Walsh, Jason, 65–67
War wounds
    described, 37–39, 50–51
    helmets and, 72, *73*
    rehabilitation, 65–67
    surgery, 59
Waters, Andre, 7–8, *8*
Webster, Garrett, 48
Webster, Mike, 47–48
Whistle-blower program, 76
Wrestling, *47*, 48
Wright, Celeste, 27

X
X-ray scans, *11*, 20–22, 23

Z
Zitnay, George, 6–7

Picture Credits

About the Author

Hal Marcovitz has written more than one hundred books for young readers. His other titles in the Diseases and Disorders series are *Blindness*, *Infectious Mononucleosis*, and *Personality Disorders*. A former newspaper reporter, he lives in Chalfont, Pennsylvania, with his wife, Gail, and daughter Ashley.